COASTAL
DISTURBANCES

by Tina Howe

SAMUEL FRENCH, INC.

45 WEST 25TH STREET   NEW YORK 10010
7623 SUNSET BOULEVARD   HOLLYWOOD 90046
LONDON   TORONTO

THE SECOND STAGE
A Non-Profit Theatre Organization

Robyn Goodman and Carole Rothman
Artistic Directors

presents

COASTAL DISTURBANCES

by
TINA HOWE

Directed by
CAROLE ROTHMAN

Starring

JONAS ABRY	**ANNETTE BENING**	**JOANNE CAMP**
TIMOTHY DALY	**RONALD GUTTMAN**	**HEATHER MAC RAE**
RACHEL MATHIEU	**ROSEMARY MURPHY**	**ADDISON POWELL**

Set Design	*Lighting Design*	*Costume Design*
TONY STRAIGES	**DENNIS PARICHY**	**SUSAN HILFERTY**

Sound Design	*Hair Design*	*Production Stage Manager*
GARY HARRIS	**ANTONIO SODDU**	**PAMELA EDINGTON**

Stage Manager	*Press Representative*
KEN SIMMONS	**RICHARD KORNBERG**

Casting by
SIMON AND KUMIN CASTING

This production of COASTAL DISTURBANCES has received special funding from the Reader's Digest Dance and Theatre Program established by the Wallace Funds, the Rockefeller Foundation, and the Ida and William Rosenthal Foundation. This production is made possible in part with public funds from the New York State Council on the Arts and the National Endowment for the Arts.

CAST

(in order of appearance)

Leo Hart .... TIMOTHY DALY
Holly Dancer .... ANNETTE BENING
Faith Bigelow .... HEATHER MAC RAE
Miranda Bigelow .... RACHEL MATHIEU
Ariel Took .... JOANNE CAMP
Winston Took .... JONAS ABRY
M.J. Adams .... ROSEMARY MURPHY
Dr. Hamilton Adams .... ADDISON POWELL
Andre Sor .... RONALD GUTTMAN

SETTING: A private beach on Massachusetts' North Shore

TIME: The last two weeks of August

ACT I   Scene 1:   Tuesday morning, around 10
           Scene 2:   Friday, noon
           Scene 3:   Monday afternoon, around 1
           Scene 4:   Wednesday, 2 in the afternoon
           Scene 5:   Friday, end of the day

ACT II   Scene 1:   Dawn, the next morning
           Scene 2:   Several hours later
           Scene 3:   The next day, Sunday, around noon
           Scene 4:   Monday, mid-afternoon
           Scene 5:   Tuesday, near dusk

There will be one intermission

5

CIRCLE IN THE SQUARE THEATRE

36th Anniversary Season

CIRCLE IN THE SQUARE THEATRE

THEODORE MANN
Artistic Director

PAUL LIBIN
Producing Director

is proud to present

THE SECOND STAGE PRODUCTION OF

TINA HOWE'S

COASTAL DISTURBANCES

starring

ANNETTE BENING   **TIMOTHY DALY**   **ROSEMARY MURPHY**   **ADDISON POWELL**

JEAN DE BAER   **RONALD GUTTMAN**   **HEATHER MAC RAE**

JONAS ABRY   **ANGELA GOETHALS**

Scenery
BOB SHAW

Lighting
DENNIS PARICHY

Costumes
SUSAN HILFERTY

Sound
GARY HARRIS

Hair
ANTONIO SODDU

Production Manager
MICHAEL F. RITCHIE

Production Stage Manager
PAMELA EDINGTON

Directed by

CAROLE ROTHMAN

This production is made possible, in part, with public funds from The New York State Council on the Arts.
The New York City Department of Cultural Affairs and The National Endowment for the Arts.
Circle in the Square Theatre wishes to express its appreciation to
The Theatre Development Fund for its support of this production.
Circle in the Square Theatre is a member of The League of American Theatres and Producers.

6

CAST

(in order of appearance)

Leo Hart .... TIMOTHY DALY
Holly Dancer .... ANNETTE BENING
Winston Took .... JONAS ABRY
Miranda Bigelow .... ANGELA GOETHALS
Ariel Took .... JEAN DeBAER
Faith Bigelow .... HEATHER MAC RAE
M.J. Adams .... ROSEMARY MURPHY
Dr. Hamilton Adams .... ADDISON POWELL
Andre Sor .... RONALD GUTTMAN

SETTING: A private beach on Massachusetts' North Shore

TIME: The last two weeks of August

ACT I

Scene 1: Tuesday morning, around 10
Scene 2: Friday, noon
Scene 3: Monday afternoon, around 1
Scene 4: Wednesday, 2 in the afternoon
Scene 5: Friday, end of the day

ACT II

Scene 1: Dawn, the next morning
Scene 2: Several hours later
Scene 3: The next day, Sunday, around noon
Scene 4: Monday, mid-afternoon
Scene 5: Tuesday, near dusk

THERE WILL BE ONE INTERMISSION.

UNDERSTUDIES
Understudies never substitute for listed players unless a specific announcement
for the appearance is made at the time of the performance.

CHARACTERS

LEO HART — The lifeguard, 28.

HOLLY DANCER — A photographer from New York, 24.

FAITH BIGELOW — Five months pregnant, 35.

MIRANDA BIGELOW — Her adopted daughter, 7.

ARIEL TOOK — Faith's guest, 36.

WINSTON TOOK — Her son, 8.

DR. HAMILTON ADAMS — An eminant eye surgeon, now retired, 72.

M.J. ADAMS — His wife, an amateur painter, 68.

ANDRE SOR — Owner of the Andre Sor Gallery, European born, 49.

8

Coastal Disturbances

ACT ONE

SCENE 1

A stretch of private beach on the North Shore of Massachusetts somewhere between Marblehead and Gloucester. There's sky, sand and ocean for as far as the eye can see. It's around 10 on a hazy Tuesday morning, two weeks into August. A large wooden lifeguard's chair looms in the foreground. Wearing his customary orange trunks, Leo is holding onto one of the side frets doing leg stretching exercizes. As he completes his morning workout, Holly Dancer drifts onto the beach. Dressed in a tee shirt and gauze skirt, she gazes out over the horizon eating a Milky Way. Leo immediately notices her and picks up speed on his exercices, interrupting her revery. Waves break in the distance.

LEO. Well, . . . hi there.

HOLLY. (*laughing*) Oh, I didn't . . .

(*pause*)

LEO. What a day, what a day!

HOLLY. I'm sorry . . .

(*pause*)

HOLLY.. . . . notice you. (*A silence as they stare at each other.*)

9

LEO.. Skip a day of warmups and the old muscles just cramp right up on you. . .

HOLLY. (*eyes averted*) I was trying to see if I could. . .

HOLLY. . . . make out the coast of Europe. You know . . .	LEO. GLLLLITTTTCH! Forget it!

(*pause*)

LEO. I'm sorry.	HOLLY. Nothing, nothing.

(*pause*)

HOLLY. I was just saying . . .	LEO. No, no, go on . . .

(*pause*)

HOLLY. (*laughing*) Forget it, it's . . .	LEO. Please?

(*pause*)

HOLLY. You know, how if you look hard enough sometimes you can make out the coast of Europe on the other side . . . ?

LEO. Europe?!

HOLLY. Well, not cars or people or national flags or anything . . . (*laughing*) Skip it, skip it . . .

LEO. No, no, I know exactly what you mean. A couple of days ago I could have sworn I saw an Egyptian pyramid in the distance . . .

HOLLY. (*trying to glide past him*) Well, I think I'll head on down to the . . .

LEO. (*blocking her way*) Hey, just a minute . . .

HOLLY. Oh, my pass, my pass! (*She starts fishing in her bag.*) Hang on, I've got it right here. I'm staying with my aunt. Mabel Darling. You know, the tall lady with the floppy hat . . . DAMNIT, SHE HANDED IT TO ME RIGHT BEFORE I . . . . Mabel Darling . . . she comes down with a bucket to bring home water from the ocean . . . (*plowing through her bag*) COME ON, COME ON, WHERE ARE YOU . . . ?! She likes to splash it on her legs while she sits in her garden . . . . GODDAMNIT, I JUST HAD IT!

LEO. Hey, take it easy, I'm not here to check people's passes.

HOLLY. I know the rules. This is a private beach . . . SHIT! (*She pulls out another Milky Way.*) Care for a candy bar?

LEO. No, no thanks.

HOLLY. You sure? (*She offers it to him while still plowing through her bag.*)

LEO. Look, I told you, you don't have to show me your pass.

HOLLY. (*waving it in front of him*) They're very good. I just had one.

LEO. O.K., O.K., what the hell . . . (*He unpeels it and takes a gooey bite.*) Mmmmmmm!

HOLLY. What did I tell you . . . ? (*suddenly freezes*) Hey, wait a minute. Since when has there been a lifeguard down here? This beach doesn't have a lifeguard.

LEO. (*enjoying his Milky Way*) Jeez, this really *is* good!

HOLLY. Excuse me, but since when has there been a
. . . .

LEO. All it takes is one drowning.

HOLLY. There was a drowning?

LEO. All I know is, six weeks ago somebody tells me . . .

HOLLY. *Here*?!

LEO. . . . this group of families near Beverly Farms needs a lifeguard until Labor Day.

HOLLY. I don't believe it!

LEO. I figured, what the hell, the fishing business has been real slow.

HOLLY. I've been coming here since I was a child.

LEO. It would be nice to take it easy at the beach for awhile.

HOLLY. My grandmother had this huge place . . .

LEO. I used to be a lifeguard in the summers. Well, I used to be a lot of things—a car mechanic, a double A ball player, a contractor . . .

HOLLY. You're sure it was here . . . ? At our little . . .

LEO. Yeah, some kid.

HOLLY. Oh no.

LEO. It really shook everyone up.

HOLLY. My aunt never told me, I guess she didn't . . .

LEO. He was real young, only . . .

HOLLY. (*hands over her ears*) Don't! (*a silence*)

LEO. Yeah, it's weird. Even though everyone knows I'm here now, not many people show up. It's like they think it's catching or something. (*a silence*)

(*FAITH BIGELOW, five months pregnant, and ARIEL TOOK suddenly appear, their two children running ahead of them. ARIEL'S carrying a mountain of stuff including several beach chairs and a battered*

*umbrella. FAITH has a neatly folded quilt over her
arm and carries a wicker picnic basket.*)

WINSTON. (*makes a bee-line for LEO's chair*) HEY
LEO, WHAT'S HAPPENING . . . ? SEE ANY
GOOD STUFF OUT THERE? . . . SEA MON-
STERS . . . SHIP WRECKS . . . ?

ARIEL. WINSTON, get down! You know the rules!

WINSTON. (*scrambling up the ladder*) HERE I COME,
READY OR NOT!

MIRANDA. (*fuming, at the foot of the chair*) No fair, no
fair!

LEO. Morning, ladies. (*WINSTON has found Leo's
whistle and begins blasting on it.*)

ARIEL. WINSTON. . . . STOP IT!

LEO. O.K. buddy, cool it with the whistle. (*WINSTON
stops, only to resume within moments.*)

FAITH. Holly Dancer, is that you?

HOLLY. Oh my God, Faith! Look at you (*She pats her
stomach.*)

FAITH. (*laughing*) I know, I know, isn't it wild?

HOLLY. (*embracing her*) Oh Faith, congratulations!

FAITH. Finally, after all these years . . . do you believe it?

MIRANDA. (*to FAITH*) How come he always get to go
up. . . .

WINSTON. (*pretending he's LEO*). Alright everybody,
clear the beach, clear the beach . . . (*He resumes blasting on the whistle.*)

ARIEL.   (*hands   over   her   ears*)
WINNNNNNNNNSTON!

HOLLY. I'm so happy for you!

FAITH. How long are you down for?

HOLLY. Only two weeks.

FAITH. How's Mabel? I never see her anymore.

LEO. (*to WINSTON*) I SAID: KNOCK IT OFF!

ARIEL. WINSTON, I ASKED YOU TO GET DOWN!

WINSTON. (*imitating LEO*) We've got some choppy looking water out there, we don't want anyone getting hurt!

MIRANDA. (*to WINSTON*) BITCH!

FAITH. (*to HOLLY*) She isn't ill, is she?

HOLLY. No, no, she just doesn't come here much anymore, she doesn't really like the beach.

LEO. (*to WINSTON*) HEY CHARLIE, WHAT ABOUT GETTING DOWN SO I CAN GO TO WORK?

HOLLY. Hi Miranda, you've gotten so *big*!

WINSTON. (*still as LEO*) Well ladies, make yourselves comfortable before the tide comes in.

ARIEL. YOU HEARD HIM, WINSTON . . . MOVE! (*he doesn't.*)

FAITH. (*to ARIEL*) You've met Holly Dancer, haven't you? Mabel Darling's niece . . . ?

MIRANDA. (*to LEO*) Couldn't I go up? Just once? I've never. . . .

ARIEL. (*shaking hands with HOLLY*) Oh yes, how do you do?

FAITH. (*to HOLLY*) You remember Ariel, she was my roommate at Wellesley. She's renting the Salisbury place this summer.

HOLLY. Great! It's a pleasure to finally. . . .

WINSTON. (*scanning the horizon dramatically*). . . . OH NO . . . ! *TIDAL WAVE! MAN THE LIFE BOATS!*

ARIEL. (*to HOLLY*) Excuse me a sec . . . . WINSTON, IF YOU'RE NOT DOWN HERE BY THE

COUNT OF THREE, I'M COMING UP AFTER YOU!
(*to HOLLY*) I'm sorry . . .

FAITH. (*to ARIEL*) Holly practically grew up on this
beach. Her grandmother had a place down here. She's
been coming every summer since . . .

ARIEL. (*to WINSTON*) ONE. . . .

MIRANDA. I HATE YOU WINSTON, I *REALLY*
HATE YOU!

ARIEL. (*to HOLLY*) How long are you here for?

LEO. WINSTON, DID YOU HEAR YOUR
MOTHER?

HOLLY. Just two weeks.

ARIEL. (*not hearing*) I'm sorry?

HOLLY. I said, only . . .

MIRANDA. (*to WINSTON*) BITCH! BITCH! BITCH!

FAITH. Look, if you're going to call him names, at least
use the right gender. It's not "bitch", but "bastard!"

HOLLY. . . . two. . . .

MIRANDA. BASTARD!

ARIEL. (*to WINSTON*) TWO. . . .

FAITH. (*to HOLLY*) And how's wicked New York
City! (*to ARIEL*) She grew up in New York City, can you
believe it? I mean, imagine *living* in New . . .

LEO. (*to HOLLY*) So, you're from New York, are
you?

HOLLY. Sorry . . . ?

FAITH. (*to ARIEL*) Her father's head of a big publish-
ing company. I'm sure you've heard of it . . .

ARIEL. THREE! ALRIGHT WINSTON, I'M COM-
ING UP AFTER YOU! (*She doesn't move. A silence. to
HOLLY*) I'm sorry, he's just got alot of energy. . . .

LEO. (*bounding up the steps*) O.K., BUSTER, SAY
YOUR PRAYERS!

WINSTON. (*stops his blasting and begins laughing with*

apprehension) HELP . . . HELP. . . . HELP!

ARIEL. (*to HOLLY*) You know boys. . . . So, how long are you down for?

HOLLY. Not that long. Only two. . . .

LEO. (*slings WINSTON over his shoulder and starts climbing down the ladder*) NO SUDDEN MOVES NOW, CHARLIE!

WINSTON. (*laughing wildly*) HELP . . . HELP. . . . HELP!

FAITH. (*to HOLLY*) We'll have to catch up later.

WINSTON. PUT ME DOWN! PUT ME DOWN!

LEO. (*sets him next to ARIEL*) Here you go, he's all yours!

MIRANDA. (*to WINSTON*) Bastard!

WINSTON. Bitch!

ARIEL. (*shaking him by the arm, out of control*) NEXT TIME YOU DO AS I SAY WHEN I SAY IT. DO YOU HEAR ME?

WINSTON. Ow, ow, ow.

ARIEL. *I asked you a question!*

WINSTON. O.K., O.K., I'll be good. (*silence*)

FAITH. Well, what do you say we head for our spot? Come on, Miranda, get your stuff. (*to HOLLY*) Please give Mabel my love. (*they head on down the beach*)

HOLLY. I will.

MIRANDA. (*quietly to FAITH*) Why do you always have to invite them? They ruin everything.

ARIEL. (*to WINSTON*) NO SWIMMING FOR YOU TODAY!

FAITH. Honey, you know what I told you.

MIRANDA. But still . . .

FAITH. No "but still's". I'm doing it for Ariel. She's had a rough time.

ARIEL. (*over her shoulder to HOLLY*) Nice meeting you.

HOLLY. Same here.

ARIEL. (*to WINSTON*) You're not setting foot in that water, do you hear me? (*They all trudge off to their spot. Silence.*)

LEO. (*to HOLLY*) Well, it looks as if it's going to be another beautiful day.

HOLLY. God, I love this beach.

LEO. The fog's burned off.

HOLLY. It never changes.

LEO. I wasn't sure whether . . . So, how long are you down for! (*a silence*)

HOLLY. (*lost*) I'm sorry.

LEO. I was just wondering how long you're planning to . . .

HOLLY. Oh, Holly! Holly Dancer!

LEO. (*laughing*) No, no, I asked.

HOLLY. I'm visiting my aunt, Mabel Darling. The tall lady that comes down to . . .

LEO. You know, you have amazing eyes. (*a silence*)

HOLLY. (*moving away from him*) Well, I guess I'll be heading on down to the . . .

LEO. (*grabbing her arm*) Wait! (*HOLLY gasps and draws back, wide-eyed. Quickly dropping her arm.*) I'm sorry. (*She stares at him.*)

LEO. I was just wondering how long you were . . . Hey, hey, it's no big deal. (*HOLLY looks more and more upset.*)

LEO. (*moving closer to her*) What's wrong? . . . Is something the matter?

BLACKOUT

SCENE 2

Friday, around noon. It's a gorgeous sunny day. LEO'S

up in his chair working on his tan; arms and legs outstretched glistening with baby oil. FAITH and ARIEL are also out with their children. FAITH is sunning herself; ARIEL is crocheting something wildly colored and beautiful. WINSTON and MIRANDA are making sand castles. WINSTON'S is a huge formless mess. MIRANDA has a turreted plastic mold, so she turns out perfect tower after perfect tower. Also on the beach is M.J. ADAMS, who's created an entire home away from home complete with quilted flooring, oversize umbrella, roomy but creaky reclining chairs, food, cold drinks, extra blankets. She sketches on a water color pad, wearing a wide brimmed hat to keep the sun out. For the moment all one can hear is the rapid scratching of her pencil.

M.J. ADAMS. (*after a furious assault, to herself*) Rats! Why won't anything hold still? (*She erases vigorously and starts up again.*)

DR. HAMILTON ADAMS. (*her husband, soundlessly approaches from the shoreline. He's wearing a beat up Brooks Brothers short sleeved shirt over ancient trunks. He's in very good shape. He dumps a stream of shells onto the quilt.*) Treasures from the deep . . . (*then sinks down into his chair with a deep sigh*) (*silence as M.J. keeps sketching*)

M.J. How was the water? It looks cold.

HAMILTON. 65. (*M.J. shudders. HAMILTON hiding something behind his back.*) I've got something for you.

M.J. (*attacks her sketch with the eraser again*) GODDAMNIT, WHY DOES EVERYTHING HAVE TO KEEP MOVING?

HAMILTON. Because we're outdoors.

M.J. (*yelling at the vista*) COME ON. . . . HOLD STILL, FOR CHRISTSAKES! (*She attacks her sketch again, growling.*)

HAMILTON. (*thrusts two closed fists in front of her*) Which hand?

M.J. You and your shells!

HAMILTON. It's not a shell.

M.J. Sponge, then . . . . Honestly, Hammy, a man of your age still picking up shells and things on the beach . . .

HAMILTON. It's *not* a sponge.

M.J. Star fish then . . . . sand dollar, whatever!

HAMILTON. (*opening his hand*) Look!

M.J. Really, darling, a person would think you'd have better things to do with your time.

HAMILTON. (*hands it to her*) Gently, gently . . .

M.J. What is it?

HAMILTON. Well, look at it!

M.J. But I'm doing something else now.

HAMILTON. Come on, just a tiny . . . .

M.J. (*looks at it, sighing*) Plus ça change, plus c'est la même chose.

HAMILTON. Well, what do you think?

M.J. Darling, I can't tell what this is.

HAMILTON. Use your imagination.

M.J. It looks like waterlogged packing material.

HAMILTON. It's a piece of brain coral.

M.J. (*quickly hands it back*) Uuugh!

HAMILTON. Isn't it beautiful?

M.J. Hammy, it's perfectly obscene and you know it!

HAMILTON. Its natural habitat is along the gulf coast . . . (*M.J. shudders again*) It's amazing it washed this far north.

M.J. (*looking out over the ocean*) Damned wind keeps shifting!

FAITH. (*rising*) I don't know about you, but I could use a little exercise.

ARIEL. (*following her off the beach*) Race you to Gloucester.

HAMILTON. (*glancing over M.J.'s shoulder*) Oh, that's very nice, dear. Very nice.

M.J. It's God-awful, and you know it!

HAMILTON. You've gotten the shoreline very well.

(*HOLLY steps onto the beach. She's wearing a battered cap, tee shirt and short shorts. She carries a large canvas bag. Eyeing LEO, she hangs back behind his chair so he won't see her*)

M.J. (*erasing again*) Rats!

HAMILTON. You're a cracker jack at composition.

M.J. (*recoils from him and rips the sketch out of the pad, scrunching it into a ball*) HAMMY, I'VE ASKED YOU *NOT* TO WATCH ME AS I WORK! YOU KNOW HOW DISTRACTING IT IS!

HAMILTON. (*putting his and on her arm*) M.J. . . . . M.J.. . . .

M.J.. (*bolts out of her chair and heads for the shore*) I'm taking a walk!

HAMILTON. I wish you wouldn't be so hard on yourself. You're really awfully good you know. M.J.? M.J. . . . ? (*She storms out of view. HAMILTON watches her go and then settles into his chair, fondling his piece of brain coral. HOLLY steps forward a few steps and rips open a bag of M&Ms. She pops them in her mouth while gazing out over the horizon.*)

LEO. Well, well, long time, no see.

HOLLY. Oh, hi. (*Rattling her candy*) Care for some M&Ms?

LEO. Where have you been?

HOLLY. What a day! Do you believe this air? (*She inhales deeply while downing more M&Ms, then heads towards the water.*) Well, see ya.

LEO. (*Rising,*) Hey, wait a minute. (*HOLLY slings down her canvas bag at the water's edge. She sits for a moment drinking everything in and finishing off her M&Ms. She then rises, reaches into her bag and pulls out a folding tripod. She tries to set it up, but the legs keep jamming. She struggles with it, getting angrier and angrier.*)

HOLLY. DAMNED TRIPOD, WHAT'S WRONG WITH YOU . . . ! OPEN! . . . . COME ON . . . OPEN! . . . . . . ARRGGGGH! (*LEO watches her with amusement.*)

HOLLY. WILL YOU OPEN FOR CHRIST-SAKES . . . ? (*She struggles with it, then has a temper tantrum and starts kicking it all over the sand.*) SON OF A BITCH . . . OPEN! . . . WHAT'S WRONG WITH YOU . . . ? GODDAMNED PIECE OF SHIT . . . ! (*She glares at it, then calmly walks over to LEO'S chair.*) Excuse me, I was wondering if you could help me with my . . . FRIGGING TRIPOD!

LEO. Easy, easy . . .

HOLLY. The lousy thing won't open.

LEO. (*Bounding down his chair*) So I noticed. (*They head down the beach together.*)

HOLLY. I don't know what's wrong with me lately, I can't seem to do anything right!

LEO. So, you're a photographer?

HOLLY. I'm having a breakdown.

LEO. Now, now . . . (*He picks up the tripod and dusts it off.*) O.K. let's see what we have here.

HOLLY. A total, complete breakdown.

LEO. My brother Butchie used to have one of these. He was really good. Especially with candid shots.

HOLLY. I can't handle my equipment, I can't set up a decent shot. . . .

LEO. There's this great one he did of a kid with a frog . . .

HOLLY. I can't even hold the camera steady.

LEO. I don't know how he got it, but the frog was sitting on the kid's head looking right into the camera.

HOLLY. It's very depressing.

LEO. The kid had this idiotic grin on his face . . . It sounds stupid, but the frog had exactly the same expression. I'm telling you, that picture could have won a contest. (*He opens the tripod in one fluid move and hands it to her.*) Here you go.

HOLLY. (*takes it absent mindedly*) Oh, thanks. (*She just stands there, staring at Leo's body*)

LEO. Well, you're all set. (*a silence*) Aren't you going to use it?

HOLLY. (*startled*) What?

LEO. I said, aren't you going to . . . (*gesturing towards the tripod*) You know . . .

HOLLY. Oh, oh, right. Thanks alot. (*another silence*)

LEO. Are you alright? (*HOLLY sighs deeply*)

LEO. What's wrong?

HOLLY. (*to herself*) I don't know, maybe it's time to move on.

LEO. I beg your pardon?

HOLLY. I can't keep doing nudes for the rest of my life.

LEO. You do, uh . . .

HOLLY. I mean, after awhile there's only so much you can say about the . . .

LEO. (*inadvertantly brushing close to her*) Nudes . . . ?!

HOLLY. (*Jumping back as if singed*). . . . human
body . . .

LEO. Woops, sorry . . .

HOLLY. God, you're so . . .

LEO. Right, a body's just a body!

HOLLY. . . . . *tan!*

LEO. I mean, what's the big deal . . . ?

HOLLY. I've never seen such a . . .

LEO. Everybody's got one! (*He laughs too heartily.*)

HOLLY. (*weakly*) . . . color . . . !(*silence*)

LEO. And just who do you get to um . . . *pose*?

HOLLY. I just finished this series of myself. It was
really . . .

LEO. (*in a tiny voice*) Yourself . . . ?

HOLLY. (*in control again*) Yeah, it's weird, but sooner
or later anyone who's into nudes ends up doing themselves. It's just one of those progressions.

LEO. But how do you. . . . I mean. . . .

HOLLY. It's really not that different.

LEO. . . . set everything up?

HOLLY. You just feel a little stupid running around
stark naked.

LEO. I mean, it must be tricky trying to pose and . . .

HOLLY. Well, you do a timed exposure of course.

LEO. Yeah, of course, I was just wondering how
you. . . .

HOLLY. (*dancing around him*) You have to be fast on
your feet, that's all. I mean, there are alot of hilarious
takes you wouldn't want anyone to see, believe me.

LEO. I believe you, I believe you!

HOLLY. But when it works, there's nothing like it.
There's something about facing your own body
that's . . . I don't know . . .

LEO. (*more and more undone*) Yeah, it must be . . .

HOLLY. It's exhilerating. (*thrusting out her arms*) I mean, there you are just. . . .

LEO. (*oogling her*) I can imagine.

HOLLY. (*realizing what she's doing, quickly recovers*) Well, another perfect day, do you believe it? (*She laughs a bit too heartily.*) (*a silence*)

LEO. Oh, your tripod. (*He offers it to her again.*)

HOLLY. Oh, thanks, (*She takes it and starts setting up her camera.*)

LEO. (*following her*) Me, I can't stand having my picture taken. Ever since I was little, I've hated it. My baby pictures stop once I was old enough to crawl. I ducked out of view for all my homeroom pictures in grade school, and in high school, I left my yearbook page blank.

HOLLY. Yeah, I'm the same way really.

LEO. Now, a movie camera doesn't bother me. It's strange.

HOLLY. (*adjusting the tripod and looking through her viewfinder*) I'm determined to photograph this beach!

LEO. (*blocking her view*) Sorry, sorry. . . . Put me in front of a Super 8 and forget it! (*He does some spirited hijinks, almost knocking her tripod over.*) Oh, sorry . . .

HOLLY. I don't know, I've been having a tough time lately. Well, when am I *not* having a tough time . . . ? With my work, I mean. I've been trying too hard. You know when everything comes out too perfect?

LEO. (*faking it*) Oh yeah. . . .

HOLLY. When result takes over intention? I'm hoping to regroup here. You know, relax a little. Take in more of the world — sandpipers, jelly fish, hermit crabs. Or at least take some pictures of other *people* for a change — widen my focus for God's sake . . . !

(*WINSTON and MIRANDA suddenly come running over to them*)

WINSTON. Hey, whatcha doing?

LEO. (*trying to ward them off*) Not too close now.

HOLLY. Setting up my camera.

MIRANDA. I've got a camera, a discomatic.

WINSTON. (*trying to crowd in*) Can I look? Can I look?

HOLLY. Sure, just don't make any sudden moves.

WINSTON. (*peering through the viewfinder*) HEY, NEATO, THERE'S A LITTLE BULLSEYE IN THE MIDDLE OF THE PICTURE.

MIRANDA. Let me see, let me see!

LEO. Easy, easy. . . .

WINSTON. (*pushing her away*) BACK OFF, MIRANDA, I GOT HERE FIRST!

LEO. Come on kids, watch it.

MIRANDA. (*starts posing like a model*) Hey. . . . do me!

WINSTON. Woa, Mandy, way to go! (*pretending he's a photographer*) Nice . . . nice . . . Now give me a little profile . . . that's it . . . and let's see some leg. . . . great! (*Her posing becomes more antic.*)

LEO. (*steadying the wobbling tripod*) She said, no. sudden. moves!

WINSTON. (*runs to HOLLY and pulls on her arm*) Hey, take our picture together!

MIRANDA. (*also pulling on her*) Please . . . ? Pretty please?

WINSTON. Just one?

LEO. Look kids, she didn't come here to . . . (*the kids began posing*).

HOLLY. (*going to her camera*) It's O.K., this is the sort of thing I do to make a living.

WINSTON. (*upstaging Miranda*) Hey everybody, look at me!

MIRANDA. WINSTON. . . . STOP IT!

HOLLY. (*clicks away, entering the spirit*) No, that's good, keep it up. The more spontaneous the better.

WINSTON. Lights . . .   MIRANDA. OWWWW,
camera . . .   you're hurting me!
ACTION!

LEO. (*moving closer to HOLLY*) I have a boat, you know. If you ever want to photograph some beautiful scenery there are all kinds of places I could.. . . .

WINSTON. (to MIRANDA) He's got a boat. Uh-oh, you know what *that* means . . .

MIRANDA. Oh boy . . . ! (*starts giggling*)

LEO. You know, I could take you around on my day off. . . .

WINSTON. Kissy, kissy, kissy. . . .

LEO. I worked for the coast guard awhile back and could show you . . .

MIRANDA. (*sidling up to Leo, affecting a sexy voice*) "Why, I'd just *love* to take a ride in your boat!" (*She and Winston mime smooching in front of HOLLY'S camera.*)

WINSTON. Come to me baby. . . .

MIRANDA. I've waited so long. . . .

M.J. (*returning from her walk*) Good grief, what's going on here?

HOLLY. (*snapping away, laughing*) We're just fooling around.

LEO. Come on kids, knock it off!

WINSTON. (*pulling MIRANDA to him with a romantic flourish*) You're driving me crazy!

MIRANDA. Come on, Honey Lips . . . *do* it!

LEO. (*dying with embarrassment*) I mean, no big deal . . . We could head up towards Rockport. Have you ever been to Thatcher's Island or Paradise Cliffs?

BLACKOUT

SCENE 3

Monday afternoon around 1. It's nippy and overcast. It's LEO'S day off. A sign hangs from his chair that reads LIFEGUARD OFF DUTY, SWIM AT YOUR OWN RISK. FAITH and ARIEL are the only ones visible on the beach. They sit high up on the sand wearing light jackets.

ARIEL. I love it when it's like this.

FAITH. Me too.

ARIEL. No one here but the true lunatics, the certifiables.

FAITH. Speak for yourself. (*a silence*)

ARIEL. It's such a relief not having *him* around. (*glancing at LEO's chair*)

FAITH. What are you talking about?

ARIEL. He gives me the creeps.

FAITH. Gee, I think he's sexy.

ARIEL. He's so . . . I don't know . . .

FAITH. Provocative.

ARIEL. But in such a creepy way. He's always strutting around displaying himself.

FAITH. Ariel!

ARIEL. I think he stuffs himself.

FAITH. (*laughing*) Ariel?!

ARIEL. Some guys do that.

FAITH. You *are* crazy!

ARIEL. Just take a good look at him sometime.

FAITH. He's a sweet guy. He's just rather well endowed in the uh . . . hoo-hah department. (*She starts laughing again.*)

ARIEL. The "hoo-hah department" . . . ?!

FAITH. You know, the old ding-a-ling area . . . (*laughing harder*) Oh God!

ARIEL. You see, you noticed too. I mean, what's a guy his age doing here? Lifeguards are usually high school kids or college students. It's creepy.

FAITH. We needed someone on short notice, and he was available.

ARIEL. It's still creepy.

FAITH. He lives somewhere in Essex. I heard he takes people out on whale watches.

ARIEL. I heard he was a professional sky diver.

FAITH. Right, right, I've heard that too! That he's broken all kinds of altitude records . . .

ARIEL. And he also races stock cars or something . . .

FAITH. I didn't know about that.

ARIEL. Oh yes, I think he won some important race in Europe awhile back . . .

FAITH. Isn't his family in the shipbuilding business?

ARIEL. The Palme D'Or . . .

FAITH. That's a film award!

ARIEL. Whatever . . . ! He just gives me the willies the way he's always hanging around that friend of yours.

FAITH. You're just jealous.

ARIEL. Sure, sure.

FAITH. Come on, you've been separated from Fisher for almost four years now. You could use a little . . . male companionship.

ARIEL. Fisher gave me enough "male companion-ship" to last a lifetime, believe me!

(*HOLLY suddenly appears. She's wearing jeans and a gorgeous hand knit sweater.*)

FAITH. (*jumping to her feet*) HOLLY . . . (*an embarrassed silence*)

HOLLY. Oh hi, I was just . . .

FAITH. What brings *you* out this misty, moisty day?

ARIEL. (*to HOLLY*) I love that sweater!

HOLLY. Oh, thanks.

ARIEL. (*advancing towards her*) What is it? . . . Mohair?

HOLLY. Gee, I don't. . . .

FAITH. (*reaching towards them*) Great earrings!

ARIEL. (*feeling the sweater*) Yeah, that's what I thought.

FAITH. (*to ARIEL*) Look at these. . . .

ARIEL. (*touching them, surprised*) Ohhh, they're so light!

FAITH. You just can't get stuff like that around here.

HOLLY. Yeah, well . . . (*a silence*)

ARIEL. (*moving towards LEO'S chair*) KIDS, ARE YOU STILL UP THERE . . . ?!

(*A blanket covering the chair suddenly moves. WINSTON and MIRANDA erupt out from under it, giggling.*)

HOLLY. (*hand flying over her heart*) Ohhhh! You frightened me!

FAITH. NO ROUGH HOUSING NOW! WE DON'T

WANT ANYONE FALLING OFF THAT THING!
(*more giggling and horsing around. A pause.*)

HOLLY. (*starting to leave*) Well, I think I'll head on
down to the. . . .

FAITH. No, no . . . join us.

ARIEL. Yes do.

HOLLY. I don't want to . . .

FAITH. (*pulling her over to them*) Come on, I've barely
seen you this summer.

HOLLY. (*sitting with them*) Well, O.K. . . .

ARIEL. (*to HOLLY*) If you ever decide you don't want
that sweater. . . .

HOLLY. Yeah, isn't it beautiful? Someone gave it to
me. (*a silence*)

HOLLY. (*leaning over and patting FAITH'S stomach*)
So, how are you feeling these days?

FAITH. Great! You know what I keep thinking
about . . . ? How girl babies are born with all their eggs.
It just blows me away—the image of a newborn being
filled with these zillions of eggs. . . .

ARIEL. And I thought *I* was the one just back from the
funny farm . . .

FAITH. When we first got Miranda, I used to shake her
like a cucuracha to see if I could hear them rolling
around.

HOLLY. (*charmed*) No . . . !

ARIEL. (*humoring FAITH*) Alright. . . .

FAITH. No, it's really astonishing. That a newborn girl
has that child-bearing potential from the beginning.
They're sort of like those nesting Russian wooden dolls.
You open the first one and there's a smaller one inside . . . and inside that, an even smaller one, until
finally there's only one left about the size of a thimble.
"Well, this is it!," you say to yourself, idly pulling on the

top to see if it will open and. . . . BINGO! It's filled with all these little seeds with faces painted on them. When Miranda was tiny, I used to think of her as being one of those dolls . . . and *I* was one of her unborn seeds. (*HOLLY laughs softly with delight*)

ARIEL. Nothing wrong with her . . .

FAITH. No, this weird thing happens with your sense of continuity with girl babies . . . You know, the Shakers had these cradles for the aged. I've seen them in museums. They're adult size for the very old. Now that I'm going to have my very own little girl, finally be part of that biological chain, I keep imagining us fifty years from now — I'll be this wrinkled crone lying in the cradle, and she'll be the mommy — rocking me back and forth and back and forth . . . and back and forth . . .

HOLLY. (*undone*) Ooooohhhhh . . .

ARIEL. O.K.. . . .

FAITH. I'm sorry, I get carried away sometimes . . . (*HOLLY tries to hide her tears*)

ARIEL. We all have our moments.

FAITH. Miranda's almost more excited than I am. (*The kids peek out from under the blanket and then dive back under again, laughing.*)

FAITH. (*to MIRANDA*) I SEE YOU!. . . . She's amazing. She's never had any problems about being adopted. (*The children begin rough-housing under the blanket again.*)

ARIEL. Come on kids, not too wild now!

FAITH. She knows how hard Charlie and I have been trying for this baby. She said the most moving thing when we told her I was finally pregnant. She said, "I feel as if all three of us made it."

HOLLY. (*enchanted*) Ohhhh. . . . (*ARIEL sighs, getting teary*)

FAITH. (*to ARIEL*) Yeah, it made Charlie cry.
ARIEL. (*hugging her, weepy*) It makes me cry.

(*HOLLY looks longingly at them for a moment, then MIRANDA and WINSTON start acting up again.*)

FAITH (*exasperated more than angry*) EASY GUYS, YOU KNOW LEO DOESN'T LIKE YOU PLAYING UP THERE!	ARIEL (*world-weary*) WINSTON . . . I ASKED YOU TO TAKE IT EASY!

(*The children quiet down.*)

HOLLY. (*rises, uneasy*) Well, I'd better be . . .
FAITH. No, no . . . don't go. (*WINSTON and MIRANDA erupt up from under the blanket again. WINSTON is now tickling her.*)
WINSTON. Tickle, tickle. . . . tickle!
MIRANDA. (*laughing and trying to ward him off*) Stop it Winston. . . . *Stop!*
FAITH. (*more amused than angry*) YOU TWO BE CAREFUL NOW, WE DON'T WANT ANY BROKEN BONES . . . ! (*to HOLLY*) Sorry. . . .
HOLLY. It must be amazing watching them grow up.
MIRANDA.   (*awash   with   laughter*) HELLLLLLLLLLP!
FAITH. Come on kids. . . . BEHAVE!
WINSTON. (*stops tickling*) O.K. Hey, Mandy, let's play a game of War!
MIRANDA. (*ecstatic*) ALRIGHT . . . ! (They set up LEO'S bench and begin playing cards)

FAITH. (*to HOLLY*) I'm sorry, you know kids. . . .

HOLLY. No, no, I was just thinking how each child is really about 85 different people. I mean, the responsibility . . . ! How do you know what to do?

FAITH. You figure it out as you go along.

HOLLY. But what if you make a mistake?

FAITH. You try to be wiser the next time.

ARIEL. The whole thing is to hang in there.

FAITH. You said it!

ARIEL. (*growls with resolve*) (*a silence*)

HOLLY. (*to ARIEL*) Are you planning to have more children?

ARIEL. I'm divorced at the moment.

HOLLY. Oh that's right. I'm sorry, I'm sorry.

ARIEL. Don't be. It's cause for jubilation. (*pause*) No, my childbearing days are over.

FAITH. What are you talking about? You're nowhere near 40, even.

ARIEL. My equipment has dried up. I haven't had a period for almost two years. My shrink at "the farm" is convinced that's part of why I keep trying to off myself. You know, feelings of worthlessness and all that. Where other women's organs are chugging right along, mine are suddenly filled with dust. I'm like this walking sand bag.

FAITH. Come on!

ARIEL. Even if I were lucky enough to conceive, all I could squeeze out at this point would be a grasshopper or dragon fly.

FAITH. *Ariel?!*

ARIEL. I'm serious. I can see it now. After 10 hours of hard labor, I'd push out this small grey . . . moth.

MIRANDA. (*comes down from the chair and cuddles up to FAITH*) Hi, Mommy.

FAITH. (*hugging her*) Hello sweetheart, having fun?

MIRANDA. It's really great up there. You can see for miles. (*WINSTON suddenly climbs up onto the railing that surrounds LEO'S perch.*)

ARIEL. (*imitating the doctor who's trying to catch her flying baby*) "Well, congratulations, Mrs. Took . . . (*missing*) Shit! Hold still, damnit! . . . It looks as if you've just given birth to a healthy ring-tailed . . . moth. GOTCHA!"

WINSTON. (*is now standing tall on the railing, his arms out like a high wire artist*) HEY, EVERYBODY, LOOK AT ME!

ARIEL. (*clutching onto FAITH*) Oh my God. . . . Winston . . . !

FAITH. Oh no . . . !

MIRANDA. WINSTON. . . . WHAT ARE YOU DOING UP THERE? (*He slowly raises his arms, poising himself for flight.*)

ARIEL. Honey, please. . . .

FAITH. Winston. . . .

HOLLY. I can't look!

ARIEL. Get. Down.

MIRANDA. You're going to kill yourself someday, you know that . . . ?

ARIEL. Winston . . . *please*?! (*Everyone moves closer to the chair, spellbound with horror.*)

BLACKOUT

SCENE 4

Wednesday, 2 in the afternoon. Towering cloud formations dapple the beach with shadows. LEO'S up in his chair wearing a light windbreaker. ARIEL and WINSTON are having lunch and playing tic-tac-toe between bites. HAMILTON is at the water's edge poking around for shells, and M.J.'s doing a series of five minute water colors which she's placed in a circle around her.

M.J. (*turns from inspecting her paintings to trying to open an ancient thermos filled with iced tea*) HAMMY, WHAT DID YOU DO TO THIS THERMOS . . . ?! (*She struggles with the lid.*) YOO HOOOOO, HAMMY . . . ? Goddamnit, I told him not to get sand in it! SWEETHEART, I NEED YOU! (*She resumes her struggle.*)

LEO. (*clamoring down his chair*) Here, let me help.

M.J. (*Trying to unscrew the lid with all her might. to HAMILTON*) I CAN'T OPEN THE ICED TEA!

LEO. May I? (*He takes it from her and unscrews it in one deft move.*) There we go. (*and hands it back to her*)

M.J. (*to LEO*) Thank you very much. (*to HAMILTON*) IT'S ALRIGHT . . . I GOT IT, I GOT IT! (*to LEO*) Poor thing's as deaf as a stone.

HAMILTON. (*walking towards M.J.*) What's that? The thermos is stuck?

M.J. NEVER MIND. I JUST SAID . . .

HAMILTON. (*reaching for it*) Well, what seems to be the problem?

M.J. Nothing, darling. Everything's fine. Just. Fine. You can go back to your shells.

HAMILTON. Hey, how about a little iced tea to wet your whistle . . . ? (*Pouring himself a cup*)

M.J. (*sighing*) No thanks, I changed my mind. (*a silence*)

LEO. (*gazing at her water colors*) Hey, these are really good.

M.J. Ugh, please.

LEO. No, they are! I mean it!

HAMILTON. Yes, she's awfully talented.

M.J. I'm just a dabbler, just a dabbler.

LEO. (*reaching for one*) May I . . . ?

HAMILTON. There's no talking to her about her work.

LEO. These are wonderful.

M.J. Well, being married to a doctor all these years, I had to learn how to amuse myself.

HAMILTON. Now, now . . . (*to LEO*) Care for a spot of iced tea?

M.J. He was never home.

LEO. No, no thanks.

HAMILTON. That's not true. Weekends I always . . .

M.J. It certainly is true! You lived at that damned hospital. And when you weren't there . . . Well, let's not get into that. . . . I don't recommend anyone marrying a surgeon, I don't care how winning their bedside manner is.

LEO. A surgeon . . . ?

M.J. An eye surgeon, if you please. (*LEO shudders*)

M.J. Oh yes, he was the best.

LEO. I believe you, I believe you.

M.J. He had referrals from all over the world.

HAMILTON. M.J. . . .

M.J. Everyone wanted him. Heads of state, popular entertainers, the ladies. Oh yes, especially the ladies! (*a pause*)

HAMILTON. Eye surgery is very routine business, she likes to embroider.

M.J. Embroider, my foot! You should have seen him pop one of the Kennedy children's eyes back into its socket after it was knocked out during a touch football game with our kids . . . He just marched right out onto the lawn, scooped it up in his hand and . . . (*making a lurid sound*) screwed it back in.

HAMILTON. (*laughing*) M.J., really!

M.J. (*resumes painting*) So, I cultivated my hobbies.

LEO. How many children do you have? (*pause*)

M.J. AND HAMILTON, (*gleeful*). Nine.

LEO. Jesus!

M.J. Yes, even *our* families thought it was in poor taste.

LEO. Nine kids . . . !

M.J. Well, I had help of course raising them.

LEO. But still . . .

HAMILTON. She's a remarkable woman.

LEO. I can see.

M.J. . . . nannies and cooks.

HAMILTON. She kept us all going.

M.J. I don't know what you're talking about. I wasn't a particularly good mother, and I had no patience with your hours. Just about the only thing I enjoyed was my pathetic little scribblings, and they *are* pathetic. (*a silence*)

M.J. (*sunny again, to LEO*) Well, I guess this is hardly the sort of job you envisioned when you took it: watching over a handful of old crocks all day.

LEO. Actually, I'm enjoying it.

HAMILTON. You see, M.J., you put much too dark a color on things.

M.J. Don't you get bored? I should think you'd die of boredom.

LEO. I have my distractions.

M.J. (*throwing HAMILTON a pointed look*) Yes, what would we do without our distractions . . . ? Hammy collects shells and sponges these days.

LEO. No kidding?

M.J. Oh yes, Hammy's always been a great naturalist, had an eye for things of beauty . . . if you catch my drift . . . (*an uncomfortable silence*)

LEO. Well, I'd better be getting back to my . . .

M.J. (*laughing*) Don't get him started on the invertebrate shore life of North America, he'll talk your ear off. (*silence*)

LEO. Well, I really ought to . . .

M.J. Yes, please don't let us keep you.

HAMILTON. What a day! There won't be many more of these.

LEO. (*heading towards his chair*) See ya.

M.J. (*quite loud to HAMILTON*) What a nice young man.

HAMILTON. Well, I'm thinking of going in . . .

M.J. How does he stand it? Chained up on that chair all day long — week in, week out. He can't swim he can't read . . .

HAMILTON. M.J., not so loud!

M.J. Always the same vista, the same motley bathers, those dreadful children . . . !

HAMILTON. Well, the water's not going to come to me, that's for sure.

M.J. The monotony must be crushing.

HAMILTON. You're here almost every day.

M.J. Yes, but I don't have to be. It's my choice.

HAMILTON. Well, it's his choice too.

M.J. But I have something to do.

HAMILTON. So does he, he's protecting us.

M.J. But it must be so *boring*!

HAMILTON. In your eyes. Maybe this is just what he needs right now.

M.J. (*sighs and pats Hamilton's knee*) You're a good man, Hammy.

HAMILTON. Now, now, let's not get carried away.

M.J. No, you really are. You're much more forgiving than I am. (*HAMILTON gazes out over the horizon.*) (*a silence*)

(*Back up in his chair, LEO can't seem to settle down. It's as if their talk about his boredom has suddenly made him aware of it. He sits, then rises, pacing like a caged animal. He suddenly picks up a copy of The Boston Globe and starts flipping through it.*)

LEO. (*to HAMILTON*) Excuse me, I think I'll take you up on that iced tea, if you don't mind.

HAMILTON. Please, please. (*He pours some into the thermos top.*) M.J. makes the best iced tea on the North Shore. . . . she squeezes fresh orange juice into it. Makes all the difference, all the difference. (*He reaches the cup up to him.*)

LEO. Thanks alot, I really appreciate it.

(*LEO casually pours the iced tea into his newspaper, but it doesn't come out the other end.*)

HAMILTON. (*in a whisper*) Did you see that!

M.J. I certainly did!

(*WINSTON now watches too as LEO opens the paper showing that the tea has vanished into thin air. He then casually pours it back into his cup which he lifts towards the Adams, and then drains.*)

M.J. I'm amazed!

WINSTON. (*pulling ARIEL out of her seat*) Mom, come quick!

ARIEL. (*reluctantly following him*) Winston, what are you . . . ?

HAMILTON. (*applauding*) Why, Leo, I had no idea you could. . . .

WINSTON. (*to LEO*) DO ANOTHER, DO ANOTHER!

ARIEL. What's going on here? . . . (*laughing*) Winston?!

WINSTON. (*reaching for ARIEL'S hand*) Just watch. . . .

LEO. And now for the classic . . . Singapore Surprise! (*He makes fanfare noises.*)

(*HOLLY suddenly materializes behind the chair. She's done something to her hair and is wearing a saucy little sundress, her camera slung over her shoulder. She drifts closer and closer.*)

LEO. Watch very closely. My hands will never leave my arms . . . (*He does a dazzling sleight-of-hand trick with an enormous surprise bouquet or flock of doves.*)

WINSTON FAR. . . .   ARIEL (*enchanted*) Oh, OUT!   Winston!

M.J. (*applauding wildly*) BRAVO, BRAVO!

HAMILTON. (*joining in*) WELL DONE, WELL DONE!

WINSTON. MORE, MORE. . . .

ARIEL.   Now,   honey . . . (*eyeing   LEO apologetically*)

M.J. You could be on the stage.

LEO. Why, thank you.

M.J. I had no idea you were so versatile.

HAMILTON. He's first rate, really first rate!

LEO. (*to HOLLY*) Oh hi. . . . where have you been?

HOLLY. At my aunt's . . . (*to the ADAMS, shyly*) Hi. . . .

LEO. Boy, things must be pretty interesting over there. I mean, you spend alot of time with her, don't you?

HOLLY. Yeah, I guess I do.

ARIEL. (*pulling WINSTON back to their spot*) Come on honey, you still have half a tuna fish sandwich to finish.

WINSTON. Yukkk!

LEO. (*to HOLLY*) She must be a pretty interesting lady.

HOLLY. She is. She's wonderful! Whenever any of us are falling apart, we always come up and stay with her. She's just so . . . easy! (*M.J., HAMILTON, ARIEL and WINSTON are rivetted.*)

LEO. Falling apart . . . ? (*Everyone quickly looks away. A silence.*)

HAMILTON. (*edgy*) Well, I think I'm going to take a little stroll. (*to M.J.*) Care to join me?

M.J.. Not right now darling, you go ahead. (*She pulls out a copy of Quentin Bell's biography of Virginia Woolf and fitfully starts reading it.*) (*HAMILTON exits*)

HOLLY. Well not. . . . *falling* . . . *apart* . . . ! I mean more . . . bottomed out. You know, everything just. . . . Whssst, forget it! (*She laughs.*) Falling apart. (*lowering her voice*) You know how sometimes you see people weeping uncontrollably in the street? (*She points to herself.*) It's very scary. (*All eyes are on her again.*)

LEO. You weep in the street?

HOLLY. (*sighs deeply*)

LEO. (*impressed*) You're kidding?!

HOLLY. In the street, in the post office, at the drug store. . . .

LEO. Jeez!

HOLLY. In the garage, the garden and tool shed. . . .

LEO. The *tool shed* . . . ?!

HOLLY. I'm driving my poor aunt crazy.

LEO. (*with a smile*) So, *that's* what you do all day!

HOLLY. It's not funny.

LEO. I'm sorry, I'm sorry.

HOLLY. (*sighs deeply again*) (*A silence. LEO suddenly glowers at everyone staring at them. They all quickly look away.*)

LEO. Me, when I hit bottom, I go out in my boat.

HOLLY. Ohhhhh. . . .

LEO. (*facing towards the ocean*) It's no big deal, just a beat up Rhodes 19. I've got an outboard on back, so I can take her through the inlets out to Crane's.

HOLLY. Oh, Crane's Beach is *the* most beautiful. . . .

LEO. Well, you ought to see it when the sun's coming up. I get out about two miles, cut the motor and just drift with the sails down. Sometimes I come in real close to shore. You know how fine the sand is at Crane's. . . . Well, when that early morning sun catches it around 7:30, it's like mica city out there! You've never seen anything so beautiful. . . . I'm thinking about moving down to the Keys where you can be out on the water, year round . . . I'd like to get into the deep sea fishing business, maybe even have a spin-off with tourist cruises. . . .

HOLLY. Gosh, that sounds . . .

LEO. Have you ever been to the Keys?

HOLLY. No, but I've got a cousin who has a place in Tampa. (*pause*)

LEO. Oh, Tampa's. . . . great.

HOLLY. I've never been there but . . . (*a silence*)

LEO. I just broke up with the girl I've been living with for three years.

HOLLY. Oh God, I'm sorry.

LEO. Yeah, it's been rough. I mean, we were going to get married and everything.

HOLLY. I'm really sorry.

LEO. She said it just wouldn't work out. Three fucking years and. . . .

HOLLY. Oh God. . . .

LEO. FOOM!

HOLLY. Maybe she'll change her mind.

LEO. Linda change her mind . . . ? No way!

HOLLY. (*touching his arm*) I'm really sorry. (*a silence*)

LEO. Oh Christ, you're so beautiful, I can hardly stand on my feet. (*He rises and stumbles towards her.*) (*All eyes are immediately on them again.*)

HOLLY. (*also rising, backing away, laughing*) Hey, what are you . . . ?

LEO. (*lunging towards her*) You just wipe me out.

HOLLY. (*raises her camera to ward him off*) You're crazy!

LEO (*He starts chasing her.*) The things you say . . . your eyes and body . . . (*HOLLY starts snapping his picture as he chases her around his chair and past the other bathers on the beach.*)

LEO. You've got the most beautiful eyes!

HOLLY. Long shot of the torso . . . medium

They're transparent al- most, like looking into cel- lophane . . . And your skin . . . it *kills* me! I dream about it. Touching you. Your arms and face . . . sleeping with you. . . . (*He practically falls into M.J.'s lap.*) Sorry. . . .

shot of the chest . . . Nice! . . . Tight in on the arms. . . . God, you've got great arms, you know that? I mean, they really are *something*. . . .

LEO. I shouldn't be say- ing all this, it's just you've been driving me crazy ever since you got here . . . It's like I'm on fire all the time. It's even worse when I don't see you—If you knew how many times I've driven past your house at night trying to catch a glimpse of you. . . . Your back, your shoulders, anything . . .

HOLLY. Close in on the face . . . Great! You've got a wonderful face, fabu- lous bones . . . O.K. Hold still a sec and look at me . . . That's it . . . Just tilt your chin up a bit . . . PERFECT! . . . And again . . . NOW WE'RE COOKING . . . GREAT. . . . THAT'S IT . . . WOA! . . . and again . . . GREAT!

(*They spin faster and faster around each other.*)

BLACKOUT

SCENE 5

Friday, the end of the day. FAITH is flat out on her blanket trying to catch the last rays of the sun. ARIEL's still working on her sweater. Both have fallen asleep. MIRANDA's sitting high up on the sand talking into a soda can telephone system she's rigged up with WINSTON who's out of sight at the moment. HOLLY'S squatting several feet away taking pictures of her. LEO rises in his chair, stretches and prepares to leave for the day.

MIRANDA. (*can to her ear*) WHAT . . . ? I CAN'T HEAR YOU! WINSTON, YOU'LL HAVE TO . . . (*She starts shaking the can.*) Wait a minute, the string's come undone. (*She fixes it and yells into the can.*) HELLO, CAN YOU HEAR ME . . . ? HELLO? . . . HELLO, ANYONE THERE!

LEO. (*climbs down his chair, drifting near Holly*) Well, see you all tomorrow. (*HOLLY'S too engrossed to notice him.*)

LEO. Have a pleasant evening. (*A silence. He moves a bit closer to her.*)

HOLLY. (*feeling his presence, rises blushing*) Oh, I didn't . . .

HOLLY. . . . hear you.   LEO. I'm sorry, I didn't
I was just um . . . taking   mean to interrupt . . .
a few . . .

WINSTON. (*suddenly storms between them holding his can*) JESUS MANDY, WHAT'S YOUR PROBLEM?!

MIRANDA. (*can to her ear*) Hey, I can hear you, I can hear you. Say something else.

LEO. (*to HOLLY*) Well, I guess I ought to be getting along. . . .

WINSTON. (*grabbing MIRANDA'S can*) I TOLD YOU: DON'T HOLD IT RIGHT UP TO YOUR MOUTH!

HOLLY. (*flustered*) I was just taking some . . .

WINSTON. (*to MIRANDA*) You've got to keep it at least three inches away. Like this.

HOLLY. . . . pictures.

MIRANDA. Well, sor-ee!

LEO. (*to HOLLY*) O.K. . . . See ya. (*They exchange a long look as . . .*)

WINSTON. TESTING. ONE, TWO, THREE, TESTING. GOOD EVENING AMERICA, THIS IS WINSTON TOOK TELLING YOU ALL TO GO STUFF IT! (*shoves it back in her face*) See, it works fine. Now you try. (a silence)

LEO. Well, so long. (*He exits.*)

MIRANDA. I don't want to play anymore.

WINSTON. But it works now.

MIRANDA. I said, I'm not playing.

WINSTON. Mandy . . . !

MIRANDA. No!

WINSTON. Come on, it'll be fun.

MIRANDA. I don't want to. Leave me alone. (*She rises and starts running away from him.*)

HOLLY. Miranda!

WINSTON. (*chasing her*) Mandy . . . !

MIRANDA. I'm not playing!

WINSTON. You penis!

MIRANDA. Faggot! (*She suddenly steps on something and drops to the sand, howling.*) OW, OW, OW . . . I

STEPPED ON SOMETHING!

HOLLY. (*running over to her*) Oh Mandy . . . !

FAITH. (*waking with a start*) What happened, what happened?

HOLLY. I'm coming, I'm coming.

ARIEL. (*sitting bolt upright*) Who got hurt?

MIRANDA. (*starts to cry*) I stepped on something, I stepped on something. Ow, ow, ow . . .

FAITH. (*rushing over to her*) Oh honey . . .

WINSTON. (*trying to crowd in*) Let me see, let me see!

ARIEL. (*trying to pull him away*) Back off, Winston, you've already done enough.

WINSTON. What did I do? What did I do?

FAITH. Let Mommy look.

MIRANDA. Ow, ow, ow . . .

HOLLY. It looks like a piece of glass . . .

FAITH. Is the lifeguard still here?

HOLLY. Let me see if I can catch him. (*She runs off after LEO.*)

FAITH. HURRY!

ARIEL. What happened?

FAITH. (*on the verge of tears*) She stepped on some broken glass.

MIRANDA. Ow, ow, it hurts, it hurts . . .

WINSTON. (*trying to sneak a look*) Where is it? I don't see anything.

MIRANDA. Mommy, it hurts.

FAITH. Oh baby . . . HOW IN HELL DID BROKEN GLASS GET ON OUR BEACH?

MIRANDA. Do something.

ARIEL. You aren't safe anywhere these days.

FAITH. (*rocking MIRANDA*) We're trying to get the lifeguard.

ARIEL. A friend of mine was at a neighbor's Fourth of

July party in Ipswich and found a razor blade in their chili, I mean . . .

(*LEO and HOLLY come running back. LEO'S dressed in civilian clothes for the first time—jeans and a tee shirt. He carries a serious looking first aid kit.*)

FAITH. Here they are!

HOLLY. I caught him just as he was about to leave.

MIRANDA. (*starts to howl*) Ow, ow, it's going to hurt. It's going to hurt . . .

LEO. (*sinking down next to MIRANDA*) Hey, hey, where's my brave girl?

HOLLY. (*to FAITH*) How is she?

LEO. (*to MIRANDA*) Now tell me what happened.

MIRANDA. I was running away from Winston and. . . .

WINSTON. Don't look at *me*; it wasn't *my* fault!

ARIEL. One of these days . . .

WINSTON. Well, it wasn't.

LEO. (*to MIRANDA*) O.K., you were running and . . .

MIRANDA. (*suddenly overcome*) I STEPPED ON SOMETHING . . .

FAITH. It looks like a piece of glass.

WINSTON. Big deal, you can't even see it.

ARIEL. (*threatening*) Winston . . . !

LEO. O.K., honey, just let me look, I'm not going to touch, I promise.

MIRANDA. (*backs away, terrified*) No, no, no. . . .

FAITH. (*trying to hold her still*) Come on, he just wants to look.

MIRANDA. NO, NO, NO. . . .

LEO. (*sneaking a glance*) Oh, this is nothing.

FAITH. See, what did we tell you?

LEO. It's just a scratch.

WINSTON. Baby!

ARIEL. Can it, Winston . . . Just . . . CAN IT! (*a silence*)

LEO. (*opening his first aid kit*) All I'm going to do is spray on a little medicine to take the sting away, O.K.? (*No response*) O.K.? . . . See, here's the medicine. We just take the top off and . . . (*He sprays it into the air.*) (*MIRANDA starts to whimper.*)

WINSTON. What a baby!

ARIEL. (*grabs him and starts shaking him, furious*) WINSTON, I'VE HAD IT UP TO HERE WITH YOU! THIS IS THE LAST TIME I'M BRINGING YOU DOWN HERE! WINSTON . . . DO YOU HEAR ME . . . ?!

LEO. (*trying to restrain her*) Hey, hey, take it easy . . .

ARIEL. GET. YOUR. HANDS. OFF. OF. ME! (*LEO quickly releases her.*)

ARIEL. (*whirling around to face him*) JUST WHO DO YOU THINK YOU ARE . . . ?! (*an awful silence*)

ARIEL. Thank you. That's more like it. (*pause*)

HOLLY. (*laughs nervously*) Well. . . .

LEO. (*circling the spray can around MIRANDA like a dive bomber*) Nyyyyyyrrrrr . . . nyyyrrrrr. it's a bird, it's a plane . . . it's . . . MEDICINE MAN! (*MIRANDA starts to laugh.*)

LEO. Here he comes, faster than the speed of light with his trusty spray can. . . . Nyyyyyyrrrrrrr . . . . nyyyyyyyrrrrrrrrr . . . (*ARIEL goes off to sulk.*)

LEO. (*spraying her foot*) Take that and that and that!. DIE, YOU EVIL THING . . . ! Nyyyyyyr, dat, dat,

dat, dat, DIE! Come on, help me. We need. . . . MEDI-
CINE GIRL for this . . . (*He hands her the can.*)
QUICK, WE DON'T HAVE A MOMENT TO LOSE!
ZAP THAT INFECTION BEFORE IT SPREADS!
(*MIRANDA starts spraying her foot.*)

FAITH. Yea, Medicine Girl!

HOLLY. It's Medicine Girl to the rescue!

LEO. (*grabbing her foot*) Now let's move in for the
kill before that evil infection has a chance to
retaliate . . . (*cackling in a sinister voice*) Think you
can outsmart us . . . ? You toad, you varmint, you low
down piece of crud! Well, Buster, you've got another
think coming!

(*He sneaks out a pair of tweezers and pulls the sliver out
of her foot.*) GOTCHA, RIGHT IN THE GIZ-
ZARD! (*A thin jet of blood spurts from the wound.*)

MIRANDA. Ow, ow. . . . *Mommy!*

FAITH. Blood. . . . !

HOLLY. I can't look!

WINSTON. GROSS! (*MIRANDA whimpers softly*)

FAITH. (*hugging her*) He got it out, he got it out,
honey!

LEO. (*gently wiping off the blood and putting away the
first aid equipment*) Let's get you cleaned up here and put
this stuff away. You never know when you might need it
again. You're some brave little girl, you know that? (*He
scoops MIRANDA up in his arms.*) (*She buries her head
against his shoulder.*)

FAITH. Awwwwww. . . .

HOLLY. Ohhhh, I can't breathe. (*pause*)

FAITH. (*to LEO*) I don't know how to thank you.

LEO. Let me carry her out to your car for you.

FAITH. We would have been lost without you.

LEO. Come on, why do you think I'm here? (*He starts walking off the beach carrying MIRANDA, then pauses for FAITH who's picking up their gear.*)

ARIEL. You go ahead, we'll get everything.

FAITH. Oh, thanks alot. (*She joins LEO and MIRANDA.*) (*LEO places his hand on the small of her back and guides them off the beach as HOLLY watches, undone. A silence*)

ARIEL. Alright Winston, come on and help me pick up this stuff.

WINSTON. (*helping her*) It wasn't my fault, honest.

ARIEL. Right, right . . .

WINSTON. But it wasn't.

ARIEL. (*getting weepy*) I just don't know anymore.

WINSTON. Come on, Mom, lighten up. (*ARIEL struggles to control herself.*)

WINSTON. She's O.K. (*a silence*)

WINSTON. (*keeps gathering up their things, then walks over to her*) Hello?

ARIEL. You're right. She's O.K. Faith's O.K. You're O.K. . . . and even I'm O.K. . . . More or less.

WINSTON. More.

ARIEL. Yeah?

WINSTON. (*putting an arm around her*) Yeah, would I lie . . . ?

ARIEL. (*with a sigh*) Where would I be without you?

WINSTON. (*exasperated*) Mom . . . !

ARIEL. Sorry, it was a stupid question. Well, you know me . . . (*pause*)

ARIEL. . . . born with a silver foot in my mouth	WINSTON. . . . born with a silver foot in your mouth.

(*They exit. A silence. HOLLY sits alone on the beach, deeply affected by LEO'S gallantry. He returns and walks over to her. A silence.*)

LEO. Well, that was quite a . . . (*He moves to sit next to her.*) May I . . . ?

HOLLY. Sure. (*They sit side by side. The sun begins to set giving the sky a rosy glow.*)

LEO. Listen, about what happened the other day, I'm . . .

HOLLY. Hey, no problem.

LEO. . . . . really sorry. I don't know what . . .

HOLLY. It's O.K. (*a silence*)

LEO. I usually don't come on like that.

HOLLY. It's O.K.

LEO. If you've been with somebody a long time, you forget how to . . . You know, three years is a . . .

HOLLY. (*putting her hand on his arm*) You were really wonderful just now.

LEO. Come on.

HOLLY. No, you were. (*a silence*)

HOLLY. The way you lifted her up in your arms . . . (*LEO moves to kiss her*)

HOLLY. (*edging away*) Leo, no.

LEO. (*tries again*) Holly . . .

HOLLY. I can't. . . . (*She starts to cry.*)

LEO. (*putting his arm around her*) Holly. . . .

HOLLY. Oh boy, here we go again . . .

LEO. What's wrong?

HOLLY. Once I get started I. . . .

LEO. Hey, hey. . . .

HOLLY. I'm sorry, I'm sorry, I didn't mean

to . . . Oh God! . . . See, I'm just recovering from something myself. It's so. . . . DUMB! I mean, you lived with someone for three years . . . Talk about setting yourself up . . . ! He just owns the most important photography gallery in the city, that's all. You know, power and promises. . . . beautiful women falling all over him . . . the whole charismatic thing . . . sweeping into rooms and making everyone's heart stop.

LEO. Ah yes, there's nothing like the good old charismatic thing.

HOLLY. The sexy accent and swimming eyes . . . kissing you on either cheek . . .

LEO. The good old charismatic-kissing-you-on-either-cheek thing.

HOLLY. Lowering his voice and swearing allegiance to only you.

LEO. The good old charismatic-kissing-you-on-either-cheek-swearing-allegiance-to-only-you thing.

HOLLY. Tying yourself in knots, trying to impress him all the time. I mean, who are we trying to kid . . . ? What if the man were a chef or a jockey instead . . . ? But of course he isn't. So round and round I go, trying not to be crazy, but then he walks into the room and . . . (*She starts weeping again.*) I'm sorry, I'm sorry.

LEO. Yeah, well, what can you do . . . ? It's like with me and Linda. She keeps saying I'm too much for her, but instead of backing off, I just get crazier.

HOLLY. I know, I know.

LEO. It's a vicious circle.

HOLLY. Tell me about it.

LEO. You try and control yourself . . .

HOLLY. Forget it.

LEO. You try not to get upset.

HOLLY. Please!

LEO. You say, just wait 'til next time . . .

HOLLY. I know. (*LEO sighs deeply.*) (*HOLLY sighs deeply. A silence.*)

HOLLY. (*stretching out on the sand*) God, I love this beach.

LEO. Yeah . . .

HOLLY. It's so comforting to think it's always been here.

LEO. Mmmmm . . .

HOLLY. Before the Pilgrims. . . . before Christopher Columbus. . . . before the Indians even.

LEO. Yeah. . . .

HOLLY. It's funny, you never picture Indians being at the beach, but they must have been. Can't you just see it . . . ? Teepee cabanas dotting the sand . . . braves surf boarding on totem poles . . . squaws sunning themselves on Navajo blankets . . . (*LEO starts drizzling sand over her legs*)

HOLLY. And before them, cavemen and sabre-tooth tigers. . . . three-toed horses tiptoing across the sand like little pigs. . . . (*She makes little rooting noises and laughs.*) Ohh, that feels good. . . . You know what I read in a book . . . ? That the island of Atlantis was really inhabited by dolphins.

LEO. Come on. . . .

HOLLY. No, it's true. They used to have legs and live on land.

LEO. Sure, sure.

HOLLY. I'm serious. If you dissect a dolphin, you'll find these residual flippers tucked up beneath its stomach. They used to be legs, but when Atlantis sank, the dolphins had to go with it and adapt.

LEO. And if a cat had a square ass, it would shit bricks.

HOLLY. I'm telling you, it's a fact! Dolphins used to walk around just like people. They wore pin-striped suits and carried briefcases!

LEO. Whatever you say. . . .

HOLLY. Come on, everyone knows dolphins are more like us than any other species. So, the resemblance has slipped a little, they probably had colonies right here— on this very spot. I can feel it!. . . . They were tremendously social, you know. They loved to party. (*Leo begins burying her in earnest*) . . . During the mating season, out came the dancing shoes and there'd be this. . . . stampede down the Atlantic coast. The men, or *bulls*, I guess you'd call them, wearing seaweed tuxedos with mother-of-pearl studs, and the cows draping themselves with garlands of periwinkle and abalone . . . Don't you love it how they always call male sea animals . . . *bulls?*! "Hey, I caught me a great *bull* walrus today!" . . . "Woa, look at that *bull* manatee go!" . . . (*She starts laughing breathless from the weight of the sand.*) Oh God, I can just see it!. . . . Wall-to-wall dolphins boogying from Miami clear up to Canada . . . Thus pulsing silver tide for as far as the eye can see . . . The surf creeping higher and higher, packing them in . . . lovesick couples sinking down to the ground . . . flippers arching, backs yielding, avalanches of seaweed and sand starting to roll. . . . Boy, do I feel weird . . . (*laughing and giddy*) I'm so light-handed all of a sudden. I mean, *headed.* Lights in the head. Get it? *Head lights!* Boy, I really do feel strange . . . (*LEO, finished with his handiwork, stands over her and sings a wavering note of triumph.*)

HOLLY. (*tries to rise*) Hey, what's . . . ?

LEO. (*dancing around her*) I've got you now.

HOLLY. I CAN'T MOVE!

LEO. (*circling her, rubbing his hands like a villain*) You're mine, all mine!

HOLLY. (*struggling to get out*) LEO, WHAT HAVE YOU DONE TO ME?

LEO. (*laughing tenderly*) I wish you could see yourself.

HOLLY. It's not funny! Get me out of here!

LEO. (*starts to leave*) Well, so long. Don't take any wooden nickles.

HOLLY. HEY, WHERE ARE YOU GOING? I'LL BE EATEN ALIVE BY SEA GULLS AND HORSESHOE CRABS! (*he exits*)

HOLLY. (*her voice getting weaker and weaker*) HELP . . . Help. . . . Hellllp . . . (*A silence. then in a sexy sing-song*) LEO . . . ? Oh Leo . . . ?

LEO. (*popping back into view and settling beside her*) You called?

HOLLY. You're a real son of a bitch, you know that?

LEO. Actually, I'm a very sweet guy.

HOLLY. Sure, sure.

LEO. No, that's my problem. I just come on a little strong. But underneath . . .

HOLLY. You're crazy, you know that?

LEO. I'm a nice guy. (*a silence*)

LEO. So, how're you doing?

HOLLY. I've got an itch on my nose.

LEO. (*scratches it*) How's that?

HOLLY. Thank you.

LEO. Any time, any time.

HOLLY. Actually, you *are* a sweet guy, you just have a peculiar way of . . .

LEO. Holly, I'm falling in love with you. I don't know what to do. (*silence*)

LEO. I don't know, I can't get my signals straight. I keep thinking you feel the same way. I have these dreams and you're always beckoning to me, opening your arms and smiling. I'm so confused all the time.

HOLLY. Leo, don't . . .

LEO. No, I've got to say it. Last night you began undressing me and whispering all these things . . .

HOLLY. (*losing more and more ground*) Please. . . .

LEO. Like all that shit just now about dolphins making it on the beach. I had the feeling something else was going on. You know what I mean . . . ? That you were telling me you wanted me—all that crap about arching backs and waving flippers. I mean, Jesus Christ. . . .

HOLLY. Leo, no. . . .

LEO. So, admit it.

HOLLY. Don't . . .

LEO. Just admit it, for Christsakes! (*HOLLY sighs long and deeply.*)

LEO. Come on, what are you afraid of . . . ?

HOLLY. I'm just so. . . .

LEO. I can't take this anymore. I mean, are you playing with me or what?

HOLLY. No, no, I'm. . . .

LEO. So then I'm right.

HOLLY. Oh God. . . .

LEO. You do . . . you know. . . .

HOLLY. (*in a whisper, shutting her eyes*) Oh yes, yes. If you knew how much.

LEO. (*kneeling down next to her*) Holly, Holly . . .

HOLLY. Leo!

LEO. (*eases down over her, covering her face with kisses*) Oh baby! (*waves crash in the distance*)

AS THE CURTAIN QUICKLY FALLS

ACT TWO

Scene 1

Dawn, the next day. A fog horn moans in the distance. HOLLY sits on her blanket midst a tangle of cast-off clothing from the night before. She's wearing LEO'S lifeguard sweatshirt. He stands over her, back in his trunks. She's clinging to his leg.

HOLLY. Don't go . . . don't.

LEO. Come on, come with me.

HOLLY. But it's the middle of the night.

LEO. No it isn't, look at the sky.

HOLLY. It's the middle of the night and you want to go running.

LEO. This is the best time. Where's your spirit of adventure?

HOLLY. You're really nuts, you know that!

LEO. (*trying to pull her up*) Come on, you'll love it. . . .

HOLLY. (*resisting*) Leo . . . !

LEO. You don't know what you're missing. (*He kisses the top of her head and jogs off down the shore.*)

(HOLLY gazes after him, then flops back onto the blanket. FAITH steps onto the beach behind her. She stops, losing herself in the view, but then recognizing HOLLY, silently approaches her and touches her shoulder.)

FAITH. *Holly*, what are you . . . ? (*HOLLY sits up and screams, hand over her heart. Faith also screams.*)

58

FAITH. I'm sorry.

HOLLY. Oh God . . . !

FAITH. I didn't mean to sneak up on you.

HOLLY. *Faith* . . . !

FAITH. Are you alright?

HOLLY. (*laughing*) I haven't had a scare like that for . . .

FAITH. I'm really sorry. (*a silence*)

FAITH. So, what are *you* doing down here . . . ?   HOLLY. Well, what brings *you* down here in the middle of the . . .

(*They both laugh.*)

FAITH. I couldn't sleep. I don't know, the fog horn gets me all keyed up.

HOLLY. Me too, me too.

FAITH. It's so plaintive. Like a lost child.

HOLLY. I know, I know.

FAITH. I just can't sleep when it's on, especially these days. I drive poor Charlie crazy, so rather than keep him up all night, I just . . .

HOLLY. How *is* Charlie? I haven't seen him in ages.

FAITH. He's fine.

HOLLY. Still a banker in Boston?

FAITH. Still a banker in Boston. (*silence*)

HOLLY. (*starts moaning with the fog horn*) Where is the fog horn, anyway?

FAITH. You know, I've never really known.

HOLLY. You think it's in Gloucester?

FAITH. I just don't. . . .

HOLLY. It's probably somewhere off Little Misery.

(*She glances down the shoreline and seeing LEO in the distance, jumps.*)

FAITH. Are you O.K.?

HOLLY. Fine, fine . . .

FAITH. (*noticing HOLLY'S blanket*) Hey, I'm not interrupting something, am I?

HOLLY. (*trying to hide LEO'S clothes under the blanket*) No, no, I was just . . . God, where does all this stuff come from? I don't believe all the shit I. . . .

FAITH. (*flopping next to her on the blanket*) What *is* it about the beach . . . ?

HOLLY. You'd think I was a bag lady or something . . . (*Suddenly noticing she's wearing LEO'S sweatshirt, she whips it off and starts burying it in the sand.*) I mean, this is ridiculous. All I want to do is take a few pictures of the sun coming up and . . .

FAITH. Did you ever notice how it's always women at the beach . . . ? Women sunbathing, women teaching the kids how to swim, women strolling along the shore . . . ? *Holly, What are you doing?*

HOLLY. (*frantically trying to make it disappear*) Who me . . . ?

FAITH. Yes, you.

HOLLY. I'm not doing anything.

FAITH. You're trying to bury the lifeguard's sweatshirt.

HOLLY. (*laughing*) I am?

FAITH. (*snatches it out of her hands and holds it up*) Yes, you most certainly are.

HOLLY. Well, well, what do you know . . .

FAITH. Did you spend the night down here with him?

HOLLY. (*pulling out her camera*) See, the great thing about taking pictures at this time of day is — everything's *reversed.* The water's light and the sand and sky are dark, so your prints look like negatives.

FAITH. Holly . . . ?

HOLLY. I'm often tempted not to develop them but just mount them as they are. . . .

FAITH. Yoo hoo . . . ?

HOLLY. Boom! There's this classic beach scene with the sand and sky much lighter than the water . . . I mean, *darker!*

FAITH. Come on, I've seen how you've been eyeing each other.

HOLLY. Wait a minute, is that right . . . ?

FAITH. I don't believe it.

HOLLY. I'm all confused.

FAITH. You and the lifeguard . . .

HOLLY. That's the thing about the beach, it just . . .

LEO. (*Suddenly comes jogging into view, golden and windblown. He beckons to HOLLY.*) Hey, Holl . . .

HOLLY. (*gasps and clutches onto FAITH'S arm*) Oh God . . . !

FAITH. He really *is* something!

LEO. (*running in place*) Come on, run with me. It's exhilerating.

FAITH. I'd better get out of here.

HOLLY. (*clutching onto her*) No, no, don't go.

FAITH. (*trying to pull away*) Holly . . . ?!

HOLLY. (*laughing like a school girl*) Don't leave me.

FAITH. (*struggling to free herself, also starts laughing*) Ow . . . ! What are you . . . ?

LEO. Hey, Holl, come on . . .

FAITH. Go on, he's calling you.

HOLLY. (*clutching onto her for dear life*) Oh God!

FAITH. (*laughing harder, tries to loosen her grip*) Holly, what's wrong with you?

HOLLY. HELLLLP!

FAITH. (*laughing more and more, out of control*) Stop it!

HOLLY. (*clinging tighter*) He's just so. . . . beautiful! Whenever he comes near me, I just . . . I don't know.

FAITH. Holly, stop it, I'm going to wet my pants!

HOLLY. Have you ever felt you were standing on the edge of a very high precipice? (*They collapse onto the sand with laughter, FAITH waving her arms helplessly.*)

LEO. Hey, you two, what's going on . . . ? (*He approaches them, holding out his hand to HOLLY*) Come on, run with me.

FAITH. (*trying to rise*) Go on, go on . . . !

HOLLY. (*awash with laughter*) Save me. . . . save me!

FAITH. (*to LEO*) I don't believe this! Holly, get a grip on yourself! (*LEO grabs HOLLY'S hand and pulls her towards him in a swooning arc.*)

BLACKOUT

SCENE 2

Several hours later. The sun is up, but it's still early. HOLLY and LEO are the only ones on the beach. They sit side by side on his chair, wrapped in her blanket. They're laughing.

HOLLY. Stop, stop. . . .

LEO. Wait, it gets better.

HOLLY. You're making the whole thing up.

LEO. Listen, when I want someone, I go after

them. . . . Juanita Wijojac — Christ, I haven't thought about her in years.

HOLLY. Leo . . . !

LEO. I was 13 and she was 11. Juanita Wijojac was the most exotic girl I'd ever seen. It wasn't just her beauty, which was phenomenal — her mother was Portuguese and her father was Hungarian or something, so she had all this hair — chalk white skin and clouds of black hair. . . .

HOLLY. And she was a child prodigy . . . ?

LEO. Incredible.

HOLLY. She played the organ . . . ?

LEO. In-fucking-credible!

HOLLY. And she had an extra finger on each hand . . . ?

LEO. Several. That was her ace in the hole. I mean, when she got going on that thing, she sounded like a whole goddamned orchestra!

HOLLY. And just how *many* extra fingers did she . . . ?

LEO. It was hard to tell. They were so perfectly shaped, you couldn't . . . (*HOLLY groans*)

LEO. No, no, you really didn't notice unless you started counting. (*HOLLY groans louder*)

LEO. All the guys in school were in love with her. We used to fantasize: if she has extra fingers, what *else* does she have tucked out of view . . . ?

HOLLY. Leo, I don't believe one word of this! (*She takes a fresh Milky Way out of her bag and starts eating it.*)

LEO. We couldn't figure out what she was doing in Essex. She must have been studying with some famous organist in the area. She didn't stay long. Only a year, but

what a year . . . ! I used to climb the elm tree next to the
First Congregational Church where she practiced in the
evening and watch her. I lived in that fucking tree! On a
clear night, there were as many as 40 guys up there with
binoculars. But no one was as loyal as me. . . . It's
funny, I don't remember the music at all, and she was
really good. I mean, when she cut loose with those pre-
ludes and fugues, she practically shook the stained glass
right off the walls—those lambs and apostles jitter-
bugged like nothing you ever saw. . . . No, it was all
her—the way she hunched over the keys, how her hair
fell across her face, and of course all those flying fingers.
Sometimes I counted as many as eight on a
hand . . . (*HOLLY shudders*)

LEO. Yeah, after a couple of hours up in that tree, the
old imagination went nuts. I saw extra eyes, extra
mouths. . . . Finally, I couldn't take it anymore, I had
to do something. I'll never forget it . . . One night I was
up in my tree as usual, when all of a sudden I found
myself marching right up into the organ loft and bam—
there I was, face to face with her. She was so flushed and
beautiful, I could hardly keep my balance. . . . I
reached out to steady myself and set off this blizzard of
sheet music. She lets out this piercing scream as if she's
just met up with Jack the Ripper, I mean we are talking
disaster city here. . . . and then I notice some of her
fingers kind of . . . disappearing down into her
palm. . . . (*HOLLY shudders*)

LEO. . . . and she's wriggling around on the bench as
if she's trying to hide something.

HOLLY. Her extra leg, no doubt.

LEO. It was awful. I immediately regretted having
come, but seeing her so flustered trying to reel everything
in, just heightened my desire . . .

HOLLY. Leo, this is the most disgusting . . .

LEO. I threw myself at her feet.

HOLLY. Count 'em folks—one, two, three, four . . .

LEO. It's not funny. I didn't know what else to do. I began telling her that I loved her, that I'd always love her, that I wanted to marry her and be with her forever. But she didn't seem to understand, so I grabbed her.

HOLLY. Oh no.

LEO. I couldn't help it, she suddenly seemed so fragile. I wanted to protect her. By this time, she was screaming in every foreign language you've ever heard. The louder she screamed, the tighter I held on to her. It was a nightmare. Her heart suddenly started going crazy. It raced from her chest, to her side, down her legs, back up to her neck. I tried to steady it with my hands, but it was all over the place!

HOLLY. Leo!

LEO. Finally, some rector or deacon showed up and pulled us apart. It was shortly after that, that her family moved away. I thought I'd never recover. I mooned around for almost two years. I'll tell you one thing—she could have given one hell of a backrub.

HOLLY. (kissing him) Oh, Leo.

LEO. (pulling her close) Stay an extra week.

HOLLY. I can't!

LEO. Come on, run away with me. We'll take off in my boat . . .

HOLLY. But I have things to do.

LEO. Have you ever sailed up the coast of Maine? . . . It's unbelievable! The islands off Mount Dessert . . .

HOLLY. I'm about to start a new project.

LEO. What, taking more nude pictures of yourself?

HOLLY. (*cuffing him*) Leo!

LEO. It's a shame to waste it all on just a camera.

HOLLY. I don't happen to think working with a camera is a. . . .

LEO. I'm sorry, I'm sorry, I didn't mean it that way. I was trying to say . . .

HOLLY. Yeah, I know what you were trying to say.

LEO. Come on, take off with me. We'll sail up Penobscot Bay like a couple of early French settlers — "Passez-moi zee caviar if you please . . . pourez-moi zee champagne . . . "

HOLLY. Some of us have work to do.

LEO. "Catch zee tiny, how you call them . . . ? *shreemp* in your hands!"

HOLLY. Important work!

LEO. (*grabbing her*) "Fuck zee work, and sail with me back to zee beginning of time. I weel show you schools of singing whales and . . . "

HOLLY. Alright, alright, I'll come!

LEO. You weel . . . ? I mean, you will?!

HOLLY. Don't ask me why. It's crazy. . . . absolutely. . . .

LEO. (*suddenly flings the blanket over their heads and lunges for her*) SON OF A BITCH, YOU'LL COME WITH   ME . . . YOU'LL   REALLY   DO IT . . . HOLY SHIT!

HOLLY. Leo, what are you . . . ? Oh my God, you can't take off your clothes up here. Leo . . . STOP IT . . . Oh my God. . . .

LEO. SHE SAID SHE'D COME . . . SHE'S GOING TO COME WITH ME . . . I DON'T BELIEVE IT. I JUST DON'T BELIEVE IT! (*As they lurch around underneath the blanket laughing and trying to get comfort-*

able, M.J. and HAMILTON ADAMS suddenly appear. They creep towards the draped chair, mystified.)

M.J. (*gazing up at it*) Morning. Is everything all right up there?

HAMILTON. Lovely day out, lovely day. Not a cloud in the sky.

HOLLY. (*peeking out from under the blanket*) Oh my God, the Adams . . .

LEO. (*popping up from the blanket*) Well, well, what do you know . . . ? It's the Adams! Morning Dr. Adams, Mrs. Adams . . . (*he quickly pulls himself together*)

HOLLY. I don't believe this. I just don't . . . (*She slowly starts to make her way down the ladder still covered with the blanket.*)

HAMILTON. Well, how's the water today? It looks a bit on the chilly side . . . Well, that was some fog that rolled in last night . . .

M.J. WHAT A BEAUTIFUL DAY! We almost didn't come because of all the fog this morning. You couldn't see your hand in front of your face.

(*HOLLY is still sneaking down the ladder.*)

M.J. I told Hammy I thought we should skip it today. I can't stand the beach when it's damp and foggy. The color goes out of everything.

HOLLY. (*trying to pass by HAMILTON*) Excuse me. . . . (*She gets into a dreadful hesitation dance trying to get past them.*)

M.J. And that wretched fog horn last night . . . ! I couldn't sleep a wink! (*to HOLLY*) Sorry. . . .

(*HOLLY waddles down the beach and plops onto the sand like a deflated jelly fish.*)

M.J. I hate the sound of the foghorn, it's so mournful. It makes me want to put a bullet through my head!

HAMILTON. Now, now . . .

M.J. Well, it does. It's so damned New England! (*pause, to HAMILTON, referring to HOLLY*) Who *was* that?

HAMILTON. Yes, I was just about to ask the same thing.

LEO. Just one of the kids. (*a pause*)

M.J. Ahhhh, smell that air!

HAMILTON. Nothing like it, nothing like it.

M.J. Well, shall we dance?

HAMILTON. After you, Madame. (*They head to their spot and start setting up their gear.*)

LEO. (*clamors down his chair*) Here, let me give you a hand.

HAMILTON. That's not necessary.

M.J. We can manage.

LEO. (*taking the umbrella from them*) Please, it's the least I can do. (*He sets it up with a flick of the wrist.*) There you go.

M.J. Why, thank you very much.

LEO. My pleasure. (*He walks to the middle of the beach and flings his arms open.*) What a day, what a day . . . ! (*He starts doing torso and arm stretching exercises.*)

(*ANDRE SOR suddenly steps onto the beach behind him. He's dressed in a snazzy three piece suit and knock-out Italian shoes. He surveys the horizon looking for someone. LEO finishes his exercises and casually walks over to HOLLY. He peels aside her blanket and offers her his hand. She takes it and he lifts her to her feet. They stand close together, laughing. The moment HOLLY'S uncovered, ANDRE starts walking towards her. Unfazed by her involvement with LEO, he breaks in on them, taking her arm.)*

ANDRE SOR. Holly . . .

HOLLY. (*astonished*) ANDRE! (*Andre kisses her on one cheek.*)

HOLLY. Andre?! (*He kisses her on the other one.*)

HOLLY. What are you . . . ? (*He clasps her in a bear hug.*)

HOLLY. (*starts laughing, exhilerated*) I don't believe it.

ANDRE. I took the weekend off.

HOLLY. How did you ever . . . ?

ANDRE. (*covering her face with kisses*) Holly, Holly. . . .

HOLLY. (*laughing and crying*) . . . *find* me . . . ?!

ANDRE. You must never leave me like that again.

HOLLY. (*returning his kisses*) I've been so unhappy. . . .

ANDRE. Mon ange. . . .

HOLLY. (*Suddenly aware of LEO, turns and faces him, stricken*) Oh my God, Leo. . . . I. . . . (*LEO drops his eyes and turns his back to her.*)

ANDRE. (*holds her tighter, whispering into her ear*) Viens-toi petite . . . Tu me rends fou!

BLACKOUT

Scene 3

Sunday, noon. It's murderously hot. The beach and ocean are bleached white. The air doesn't move. Jellyfish bodies spangle the shore like mucous frisbees. During the evening a beached and bloodied whale was washed ashore. Its huge decomposing body dominates the waterfront. FAITH, ARIEL, MIRANDA, WINSTON and LEO are all standing around it. (ARIEL makes a shuddering sound)

FAITH. I can't look.

WINSTON. Far. Out.

LEO. (*pulling him back*) Come on, not too close. (*ARIEL shudders again.*)

MIRANDA. (*jumping away*) It's moving, it's moving!

FAITH. Where did it come from?

ARIEL. Ohhh, the smell . . . !

LEO. It looks like a sperm whale.

MIRANDA. EEEEEEEWWW, EEEEEEEEEEEWWWWWWWWW!

ARIEL. You never think about the smell. . . .

WINSTON. (*approaching it*) HEY, LET'S TAKE SOME OF ITS TEETH!

LEO. (*pulling him back*) I said: not too close!

WINSTON. Eben Bliss has a whole bowl of barracuda teeth. They're so neat. . . .

LEO. I've called the coast guard. They'll be by sometime this afternoon to drag it back out to sea.

FAITH. I've heard of whales getting lost and beaching themselves, I just never thought it could happen here.

LEO. I'd say this one had a run in with a few sharks first.

WINSTON. (*breaks away and starts scooping handfuls of gunk off its body*) Hey, *blubber*! Blub, blub, blub . . .

(*LEO, ARIEL and MIRANDA speaking all together*)

LEO. (*jumping on him*) HEY, HEY, HEY . . .

ARIEL. (*dragging him back*) DON'T TOUCH, YOU COULD GET A DISEASE!

MIRANDA. EEEWWWWW . . . EEEWWWWW!

ARIEL. It's full of contagion. You could catch something really horrendous!

FAITH. Come on, kids, leave it alone.

MIRANDA. (*starts dancing around the whale*) The Black Plague or Leprosy. . . . EEEEEWWWWWW, WINSTON COULD GET LEPROSY!

WINSTON. (*joins in, acting out the diseases*) Or Sleeping Sickness. . . . or Malaria . . .

MIRANDA. The Bubonic Plague . . .

WINSTON. St. Vitas Dance . . .

MIRANDA. Whooping Cough . . . Whoop, whoop, whoop . . .

WINSTON. Dropsey!

MIRANDA. Rabies . . . !

WINSTON. Oh, *Rabies*! Rabies is great! (*He scoops sand onto his face so it looks like he's foaming at the mouth. MIRANDA follows suit. They become more and more animalistic as they drop down on all fours and race around the body, barking like dogs. FAITH and ARIEL laugh uneasily, which just eggs them on.*)

FAITH. Kids, come on . . .

ARIEL. (*laughing*) It's not funny.

LEO. Knock it off! (*WINSTON barks louder and louder and wags his behind. In a fit of inspiration, he lifts his leg and feigns peeing on the whale.*)

ARIEL. (*trying to hide her mirth*) Winston . . . !

FAITH. Kids . . . !

LEO. Come on guys, show a little respect for once. (*Miranda barks louder and louder.*)

ARIEL. Winston, calm down!

FAITH. Miranda, what are you doing? (*WINSTON races over to LEO and nuzzles against his leg, yelping and wagging his behind. MIRANDA follows.*)

LEO. I said: KNOCK IT OFF! (*They pay no attention and mime peeing on his leg in a delirium of laughing and barking.*)

ARIEL (*also laughing*)   FAITH (*trying to control*
HONEY. . . . PLEASE?!   *herself*) KIDS . . . CUT
                              IT OUT . . . !

LEO. (*roughly pulling the kids to their feet and sitting them down in front of him*) JESUS CHRIST, WHAT'S WRONG WITH YOU PEOPLE . . . ?! SOME POOR ANIMAL GETS RIPPED APART BY SHARKS AND IT'S ALL JUST A BIG JOKE TO YOU . . . ! Did you ever stop to think how it might have *felt* . . . ?! To be swimming along minding your own business—what a day, what a day, oh baby, this is the life—and then BLAM. . . . you're blindsided out of nowhere . . . (*kneeling down next to them*) You think everything's just out there for your own private amusement. Well, you don't have a clue about real life. Not. one. fucking. clue!

BLACKOUT

SCENE 4

Monday, LEO'S day off, mid-afternoon. It's drizzling

and overcast. The fog horn is on. LEO'S sign, LIFE-GUARD OFF DUTY, SWIM AT YOUR OWN RISK bangs forlornly against his chair. The whale is gone. Approaching voices are heard.

HOLLY. (*strolling into view with ANDRE*) Pierro came to the show with Dina?

ANDRE. They've been seeing each other for quite some time now.

HOLLY. I don't believe it!

ANDRE. She's been invited to show at the Modern, you know.

HOLLY. The *Modern* . . . ?!

ANDRE. Her new stuff is spectacular. I hope to lure her into my next group show. Blossom, Io and Zinkaloff have already committed.

HOLLY. I had no idea Dina was so . . . And how were Haskell's reviews?

ANDRE. *Fabulous!*

(*HOLLY'S barefoot, dressed in her gauzy skirt and sweater—all in white. ANDRE'S wearing his Italian shoes and a chic raincoat. He carries an umbrella.*)

HOLLY. Well, here we are again. . . . the little beach where I spent all my summers as a child. It doesn't have anywhere near the sweep of Crane's where I took you yesterday, but . . . Are you O.K.?

ANDRE. (*fussing with one of his shoes*) So much for these shoes.

HOLLY. Take them off, you'll be much more comfortable without them. (*stooping down to untie them*) Here, let me. . . .

ANDRE. (*pulling her back up*) No, no I'm fine this way . . . Please . . .

HOLLY. But you'll be so much more. . . .

ANDRE. (*still fussing with it*) It's just a little sand . . .

HOLLY. (*bending down again*) You're sure I can't . . .

ANDRE. I'm fine, I promise you. (*He glances up at LEO'S chair.*) Here, why don't we sit up here . . . ? (*He starts climbing up.*)

HOLLY. NO!

ANDRE. Come on, I've never been up on one of these.

HOLLY. You can't!

ANDRE. What do you mean, I can't? The sign says . . .

HOLLY. You just *can't*, that's all!

ANDRE. (*climbing the rest of the way up*) But no one's here.

HOLLY. Andre . . . NO!

ANDRE. (*sits down and opens the umbrella which he holds directly over his head*) Oh, this is marvelous . . . ! (*He looks out over the horizon.*) I feel like a king! (*a silence as ANDRE freezes into a Magritte-like image*)

HOLLY. (*eyes filling with tears*) Please?

ANDRE. Quick, come up and join me. You can see for miles!

HOLLY. Andre, you can't sit up there!

ANDRE. (*stands, pretending he's a lifeguard*) What ho, do I hear cries for help?

HOLLY. Get. Down!

ANDRE. Is that a maiden in distress I see out there?

HOLLY. Andre, *please* . . . !

ANDRE. Never fear, I will battle the giant squid to its death!

HOLLY. You can't stay up there!

ANDRE. (*rising*) Alright, alright, if it means so much to you . . . Just a moment while I close this umbrella. (*He starts making his way down the chair.*)

HOLLY. Thank you. (*a silence as he walks over to her*)

ANDRE. (*kissing the top of her head*) You're such a child sometimes. I never know what you're going to do next. (*a pause*)

HOLLY. (*intense*) You know what I'm thinking of getting into when I get back . . . ? X-rays! The next step beyond nudes—actually piercing through the skin to a whole new landscape of dappled rib cages and irredescent tendons . . .

ANDRE. (*laughing*) Holly, Holly . . .

HOLLY. No, I've got a friend that works in a lab. He says he can always use an assistant. I mean, can't you see it . . . ? Mounting a whole show of pancreases, gall bladders, large intestines . . . ?

ANDRE. (*affectionate*) . . . and she's off . . . !

HOLLY. I'd turn the gallery into a kind of spook house with dim fluorescent lighting—hook up tapes of muffled breathing and erratic heartbeats. It would be like entering this night blooming garden of forbidden delights. . . .

ANDRE. (*hugging her*) What an imagination you have! No one sees the world like you. (*pause*) It's so good to see you again. . . . You can't imagine what I've been through since you left. Lydia. . . . the gallery. . . . Haskell's installation. . . .

HOLLY. Yes, mounting 2,000 polaroids can't be easy.

ANDRE. 2,500! And they had to be placed in order, just so. If so much as one print was out of sequence, he exploded and threatened to pull out. This went on every day, eight hours a day for almost a week. That's why I'm looking forward so much to doing your show. . . .

HOLLY. (*walking away, stoney*) Sure, sure . . .

ANDRE. Holly, Holly, you know what my scheduling problems are like. . . . I have long-standing commitments. Stephan's new show, Lillewasser's retrospective . . . (*silence*) Sweetheart, you know how much I love your work. You must be patient. I want to present you in the spring. Timing is so important. And you'll have more work by then. Who knows, maybe even some nudes on this beach that means so much to you. I just want what's best for you, *believe* me!

HOLLY. (*subdued*) I know, I know.

ANDRE. Holly, Holly, the prospect of driving up here to see you was the only thing that kept me going this week. You can't imagine how ghastly it's been — As bewitching as Lydia may be on a movie screen, she's something else entirely with divorce lawyers.

HOLLY. (*moving away from him*) Yeah, well. . . .

ANDRE. She wants blood. They always want blood.

HOLLY. It must be awful.

ANDRE. There's more. I have to go to Europe again.

HOLLY. Andre, no!

ANDRE. You think I want to go?

HOLLY. NO!

ANDRE. You think I enjoy these separations?

HOLLY. For how long?

ANDRE. Three weeks, maybe more.

HOLLY. *NO* . . . !

ANDRE. There's some new work in Paris and Brussels I've got to see.

HOLLY. (*running away from him*) No, no, no. . . .

ANDRE. (*catching her and wrapping his arms around her*) Cheri, tenez. . . . Let me try and explain . . .

HOLLY. No!

ANDRE. Please, it's important.

HOLLY. (*struggling*) Let me go!

ANDRE. Sweetheart . . . !

HOLLY. Andre . . . !

ANDRE. Try to understand . . .

HOLLY. (*suddenly clinging to him*) Oh Andre, I love you so!

ANDRE. Holly, Holly. . . .

HOLLY. It's too much.

ANDRE. Listen to me . . . sweetheart . . .

HOLLY. . . . . . just. . . . too . . . much!

ANDRE. Please!

HOLLY. (*sighs deeply*)

ANDRE. Once upon a time there was a man who was a diamond cutter in Antwerp, but like so many Jews, he was forced to flee his homeland at the outbreak of the war. The Nazis confiscated his entire supply of uncut gems, so all he could bring with him was his talent. I'm talking about my father of course . . . (*HOLLY nods with recognition*)

ANDRE. . . . He settled his family in Brooklyn. Life was hard because the streets were filled with refugees just like him — merchants without their wares, artists without their materials . . . In the beginning he made his living as a handyman, repairing leaky faucets, upholstering furniture, sharpening scissors. There was rarely enough to eat.

HOLLY. What did he look like? You've never really described him.

ANDRE. My father . . . ? He had beautiful hands, like a cellist. He was slim, medium height with a beard. He always wore a hat. People often said he resembled Sigmund Freud.

HOLLY. No!

ANDRE. Oh yes, he was quite imposing.

HOLLY. And your mother . . . ?

ANDRE. . . . . was very fat.

HOLLY. (*laughing*) Oh Andre . . .

ANDRE. But with a magnificent singing voice that could charm the birds right out of the sky.

HOLLY. You're so lucky, my mother can't even carry a tune.

ANDRE. Oh yes, she would have had a great career if only the timing had been different.

HOLLY. All my parents can do is play tennis. It's so boring. Every weekend they play mixed doubles with Jack and Gabby Wainwright. Jack was on the Davis Cup team back in. . . .

ANDRE. (*with gentle impatience*) Holly. . . .

HOLLY. I'm sorry, I'm sorry . . . I got carried away.

ANDRE. (*affectionately*) Holly Dancer . . . !

HOLLY. Go on . . . please . . . *please*!

ANDRE. For all our poverty and deprivation, we had two sources of great joy . . . First, was our Sunday outings to Brooklyn Heights when we'd walk out on the piers to gaze at the view of lower Manhattan. Every Sunday — spring, summer, winter, fall — my father would cry, "Forois zum wunderland!" Which in Yiddish meant, "Come to our enchantment!" . . . and we'd scramble onto the trolly car, my sisters almost trampling me under their shoes . . . My father knew the skyline by heart. As we stood there, he'd begin his litany — "There, the Woolworth Building, to its left, the Bank of Manhattan, Farmer's Trust, the Cities Service Tower, the Municipal Building . . . !" ". . . Slow down, slow down!", my mother would cry. "They'll never learn anything if you go so fast!" . . . "And over there?," he'd point — "the one with the golden roof shaped like a pyramid?" . . . "THE COURTHOUSE, THE COURTHOUSE!," we'd all clamor, eager to be the first with the right answer. . . .

HOLLY. I can just see you jumping up and down, shouting louder than everyone else. (*Thunder rumbles in the distance and it starts to rain.*)

ANDRE. (*taking her hand and heading under LEO'S chair*) Come on, let's run under here, it's starting to pour . . . (*holding her as he leans against one of the frets*) There, isn't this better . . . ? Now, our second joy, yes . . . ? As I said, my father was a diamond cutter. His gems were prized by the most beautiful women of Europe. He was a master. It was his *eye*! He could see the jewel where none existed. As a handyman in this country, he acquired boxes of cast-off junk — clock springs, sewing machine parts, glass door knobs, old eyeglasses. After a day of haggling in the streets, he'd haul out his boxes of treasures and lose himself in the minutae of small gold springs and moving parts . . .

HOLLY. You have such a lovely voice.

ANDRE. Well, three or four times a year as we were finishing our meager Friday evening Shabbas dinner, he would suddenly announce, "I have something to show you, my children." You see, my father was also an amateur watchmaker. He built fantasy clocks that played tunes instead of telling time — mechanical toys that flew around the room — ticking bifocals. . . .

HOLLY. I could listen to you forever.

ANDRE. As our circumstances worsened, his creations became even more fanciful. They reached their height the winter my sister Sophie almost died of pneumonia. Just as she was fluttering back into consciousness, my father whispered, "Ich hab epes eich zu veissen, mein kinder" . . . He reached under the bed and pulled out this crystal sphere about the size of a softball. Inside it was a miniature rendering of our cherished view — the Woolworth Building, the Bank of Manhattan, Farmer's Trust. . . . (*HOLLY gasps*)

ANDRE. But what was most astonishing of all was — he'd fashioned it as a clock with tiny numbers around the circumference. (*rotating and miming the movement*) Every hour on the hour, something within the sphere moved. At 8 o'clock, the Woolworth Building bent at the middle and doffed its roof. At 9 o'clock, one of the little barges suddenly sent off a blast of steam. At 10 o'clock, a flock of seagulls wheeled up over the court-house . . . As you can imagine, there was no sleeping that night. My father's fancy had not only animated our secret world, it also made it tangible—something we could hold in our hands. For Sophie, it was like being given back her life again. For me, it was a testament to the transforming eye of the artist. I don't have those gifts. (*pause*) I can only admire. Innocence eludes me. But you—you and my father—you walk with the angels. Think of it—living a life promoting a talent you'll never have, a beauty you'll never be able to create.

HOLLY. (*starts to weep*) Oh Andre . . .

ANDRE. Non, non petite, ne pleur pas. I accepted it a long time ago.

HOLLY. Don't leave again!

ANDRE. You give me great joy.

HOLLY. I can't stand these separations anymore.

ANDRE. Just be patient with me.

HOLLY. . . . two weeks in Europe, three weeks in South America . . .

ANDRE. We've waited so long . . .

HOLLY. Meetings in Tokyo . . .

ANDRE. Sweetheart. . . .

HOLLY. You're not listening to me.

ANDRE. You have such talent, such freshness and beauty . . .

HOLLY. I can't go on like this.

ANDRE. Your skin and eyes. . . .

HOLLY. You make me so unhappy.

ANDRE. (*holding out his arms to her*) Come to me.

HOLLY. I can't go on like this.

ANDRE. Mon coeur, mon ame. . . .

HOLLY. I just. . . . *Can't!* (*As they stand frozen in their misery, LEO suddenly appears walking along the shoreline. He sees them and stops as if hit by lightning.*)

BLACKOUT

SCENE 5

Tuesday, late afternoon. Enormous clouds hang motion-less in the sky. FAITH and ARIEL are shaking out their blankets preparing to leave. FAITH'S wearing the sweater ARIEL'S been working on all summer. WINSTON and MIRANDA are writing their names in the sand. LEO'S up on his chair, staring into space.

FAITH. O.K., kids, time to leave.

ARIEL. Chop, chop, Winston, let's get moving.

MIRANDA. Oh, do we *have* to . . . ?

FAITH. Daddy's coming home early tonight.

MIRANDA. He is . . . ? Oh goody!

FAITH. (*suddenly embraces ARIEL*) I really love this sweater you made me.

ARIEL. Oh, I'm glad. I've been on a tear lately. You should see what I've been working on at home. It started out as a shawl, but is turning into this gigan-tic . . . now, don't laugh . . . *house*! It's the damn-dest thing, but that's what it looks like. Winston and I joke around that when we get back to town, we'll actu-ally move into it.

FAITH. Ariel?!

ARIEL. He's been helping me from the start. We haven't had so much fun in years . . . ! The first floor is made out of ragg wool and hemp, the second, out of mohair and angora . . . It's so soft and spongy we laugh that if he starts jumping on his bed, he'll fly right out through the roof!

FAITH. (*laughing, shaking her head*) You two . . . (*pause*)

ARIEL. (*casually*) You really saved my life, you know. (*pause*) Well, only a few more days and summer's over. Labor Day's almost here. School will be starting soon.

FAITH. Don't . . . !

ARIEL. (*patting FAITH'S stomach*) Just think, next year at this time . . .

FAITH. (*laughing*) Oh God . . .

ARIEL. O.K., Winston, let's pack it in.

WINSTON. Wait . . . Just one more game of tic-tac-toe . . . ? (*He draws a grid on the sand.*)

ARIEL. (*affectionately*) You loon!

WINSTON. Please?

ARIEL. O.K., but it better be quick. (*She places an 0 in the upper left-hand corner.*) (*WINSTON places an X in the upper right-hand corner.*) (*ARIEL places an 0 directly beneath her first one.*)

WINSTON. (*puts an X in the bottom left-hand corner, then draws a line through them.*) I won, I won!

ARIEL. No fair, I'm hopeless at tic-tac-toe.

FAITH. (*starting to trudge off the beach with MIRANDA*) Come on guys, it'll be dark soon.

WINSTON. I'm just smarter than you, that's all.

ARIEL. You are smarter than me, come to think of it. That's always been the trouble between us.

WINSTON. Come on, I'm not *that* smart . . . !

ARIEL. No, you are. You're very quick. You're going to be a great man someday.

WINSTON. Jeez, you really *have* flipped your lid!

ARIEL. No, I'm serious. You've got alot of spirit. Spirit counts for everything in this world!

WINSTON. (*suddenly looks up at her*) Race you to the car. . . .

ARIEL. (*not in the mood*) Winston. . . .

WINSTON. Come on, one last time . . . ? (*a pause as she stands looking at him. Without warning she sprints off ahead of him.*)

WINSTON. (*struggling to catch up*) Hey, no fair . . . no fair. You got a head start. . . . Mom . . . ! (*and they're gone. A stillness descends. LEO stretches and looks at his watch. He starts getting ready to leave for the day.*)

HOLLY. (*suddenly comes teetering onto the sand in high sling-back sandals and a jump suit. She stands slightly behind LEO'S chair, gazing out over the ocean. She stumbles closer.*) Hi . . . (*pause*) I wanted to stop by and see you before I. . . . Boy, the place is really deserted. You know in the old days the beaches around here used to be jammed . . . I'm talking thousands . . . *millions* of people . . . At the turn of the century they had these special trollies from Boston. . . . Revere Beach . . . ? You wouldn't believe it! Miles of boardwalk . . . dance halls . . . amusement palaces . . . diving horse acts . . . fireworks . . . ! (*She starts to lose her balance and grabs onto his chair.*) WOOPS!

LEO. (*pulling on his jeans*) So, you're going back . . . ?

HOLLY. I'm not used to wearing heels on the beach.

LEO. When are you leaving?

HOLLY. You know, all this time and I never took a

picture of your chair. Do you believe it? I mean, of all the things to. . . . (*She falls again.*) Oh God!

LEO. (*starts scrambling down the ladder to help her, but suddenly slips on something and pitches into the sand*) SON OF A BITCH!

HOLLY. (*crawling over to him*) Are you alright? (*For a moment, both are on their hands and knees, desperately trying to stand up.*)

LEO. One of the kids left their fucking shovel on the steps! (*He brandishes it in one hand.*)

HOLLY. (*trying not to laugh*) I'm sorry.

LEO. STUPID IDIOTS!

HOLLY. How do you stand it?

LEO. I don't, but I've only got a couple of days to go, so what the hell.

HOLLY. Then what will you do?

LEO. (*turning the shovel in his hands*) I don't know . . . I'd really like to try and make it down to the Keys, but I've got to get my hands on some money first. I have a friend who wants me to manage a seafood chain in Rockport. The money's real good, but I hate working indoors. I don't know, maybe I'll see what's going on in the construction business. (*He absent-mindedly hands her the shovel.*)

HOLLY. Yeah, I hear you can make a fortune in it— $1,000 a day or something. . . . and you don't have to show up when the weather's bad . . . there are all kinds of kick-backs and overtime bonuses . . . I don't know what I'm talking about. (*a silence*)

LEO. How can you stand that guy?

HOLLY. (*handing the shovel back to him*) Here, I don't want this.

LEO. He's such a phony. He'll fucking eat you

alive. . . . ! Look, I know it's none of my business, but
you're throwing yourself away—and for what . . . ?
Some mythical show he keeps promising you. . . .

HOLLY. Listen, I didn't come here to be lectured
about. . . .

LEO. O.K., O.K. . . . . . . (*a silence*)

LEO. He's just such an operator. I know the type. All
talk. I bet he wears a diamond pinkie ring.

HOLLY. (*tries to set out again, wobbly*) I assure you,
he's never even *seen* a . . .

LEO. . . . and $60 cologne with names like "Whip"
or "Surrender" . . . (*grabs her hand and leads her to
the ladder of his chair*) You know, you'd have a much
easier time if you took those off.

HOLLY. (*sitting with a thud*) Shit! (*LEO squats beside
her and starts undoing one of her sandals.*)

HOLLY. What are you doing?

LEO. Taking off your shoes. Come on, hold still.

HOLLY. (*moving her foot away*) Who said anything
about taking off my shoes!

LEO. You keep falling down.

HOLLY. It has nothing to do with my shoes.

LEO. (*trying to grab her foot*) Will you hold
still . . . ?

HOLLY. Look, Leo. . . .

LEO. (*struggling with her*) Come on. . . .

HOLLY. I know it looks bad with Andre, it *is* bad with
Andre. He makes me crazy, but I'm just so alive with
him. I can't explain.

LEO. And with me, you're only happy, right . . . ?
(*pause*) You're a real ass hole, you know that? (*a
silence*)

HOLLY. I knew this was a mistake. I knew I shouldn't

have . . . (*She tries to walk again, but promptly falls.*)
WOOPS!

LEO. Look, if you took off those shoes. . . .

HOLLY. (*scrambling to her feet*) I TOLD YOU: IT
HAS NOTHING TO DO WITH MY GODDAMNED
SHOES! IT'S YOU . . . ! (*She pulls them off, takes a
few tentative steps and immediately falls*) See . . . ? It's
you. . . . There's only one way to do this . . . (*She
hands him her shoes*) Here . . . Stand Back . . . !
(*She drops to her hands and knees and starts crawling off
the beach*)

LEO. (*approaching her*) Holly, what the hell are
you. . . . ?

HOLLY. I said: STAND BACK! (*He does. A silence*)

HOLLY. (*inching forward again*) This may not be the
most dignified exit in the world, but at least I'm moving . . . The trick is to stay away from you. It's like
you're electrified or something. Everytime you come
near me I . . . (*She makes sizzling and crackling
sounds.*)

LEO. (*immediately touches her*) Holly . . .

HOLLY. (*starts laughing*) See . . . ? Oh boy, here we
go . . . ! Listen, I had a wonderful time with you, really
wonderful. . . .

LEO. I don't believe this.

HOLLY. (*crawling faster and faster*) I *knew* this would
happen, I *knew* I shouldn't. . . .

LEO. (*has also dropped to all fours, chasing her*) Jesus,
will you. . . .

HOLLY. It wouldn't work and you know it!

LEO. (*trying to catch her*). . . . slow down?

HOLLY. Come on, let me go. . . . I'd never get anything done with you around. You'd always be sneaking

up on me with that look in your eye — pulling the camera out of my hands and grabbing me in the dark room. I know you . . . ! You have no idea how ferocious I get when I can't do my work . . . I mean, I get nasty! I snap at the mailman, I push old ladies down in the supermarket, I'm a real . . .

LEO. (*tackles her*) Gotcha!

HOLLY. (*goes sprawling*) . . . monster! (*struggling to free herself*) Leo, please . . . ! I'd drive you crazy . . . ! I'm a terrible housekeeper, I don't know how to cook, I forget the days of the week, I'm moody . . . Oh, am I moody! When I get stuck on something, forget it! (*She starts to cry.*) Leo, please . . . he's picking me up in just a few minutes. . . .

LEO. (*pinning her*) Don't go. Don't . . . (*a silence*)

HOLLY. I could never live in the Keys. It sounds so scarey. Deep sea fishing, people tearing around in motorboats. I mean, what would I do there?

LEO. Hey, hey, slow down. Nobody said anything about . . .

HOLLY. Take those dopey pictures of tourists holding up 10 ton dead tunas they just caught . . . ?

LEO. I just want to see you again.

HOLLY. "Hey, you in the Hawaiian shirt, want to move that tuna a little to the left, it's blocking your wife!"

LEO. Come on, give me your address and phone number in the city.

HOLLY. "Great! Now smile! Not the fish . . . *you*!" Actually, I'd probably make alot more money than I do now. . . .

LEO. (*starts going through her bag*) You must have a pencil and piece of paper in here . . . (*candy bars start spilling out*) What have you got in here? A goddamned candy store?!

HOLLY. Leo, what are you . . . ?

LEO. (*pulling out a pencil and piece of paper*) Ah, here we go. . . . Can I use this?

HOLLY. (*snatching the piece of paper*) What *is* that?

LEO. How should I know, it's your . . .

HOLLY. Wouldn't you know it — it's the invitation to Haskell's opening — lucky bum! (*She thrusts it at him in disgust.*)

LEO. O.K., shoot!

HOLLY. Leo, I really don't think this is a very good . . .

LEO. Come on, cough it up.

HOLLY. I mean, it would be so strange to see you in the city.

LEO. Let's go.

HOLLY. Alright, alright . . . (*mumbling, inaudible*) 197 East 4th Street . . .

LEO. I beg your pardon?

HOLLY. I said: 197 East 4th Street. Oh God, I don't believe I . . .

LEO. And your number . . . ?

HOLLY. (*resumes crawling away from him, very fast*) Look, I really think this is . . .

LEO. (*following on his hands and knees*) Yes . . . ?

HOLLY. (*inaudible*) 212-533-0749 . . . Holly, what *are* you doing . . . ?!

LEO. (*trying to keep up with her*) 212 . . . what?

HOLLY. (*going faster and faster*) 533-0749. . . . (*She starts laughing and talking to herself.*) You've really flipped your . . . (*She suddenly bumps smack into the ADAMS who soundlessly appear in her path carrying folding chairs, a small table, a mysterious white beach umbrella, a bolt of gauzy material and party stuff in their picnic basket. HOLLY screams at the impact.*)

M.J. (*also screams, jumping back*) Holly Dancer, is that you?!

HOLLY. (*still on all fours*) Oh, hi Mrs. Adams, I was just. . . .

LEO. (*writing it down*) 197 East 4th Street. . . .

HAMILTON. (*to HOLLY*) Well, well, don't you look attractive.

LEO. 212-533-0749.

M.J. Did you lose something?

HOLLY. (*finally rises and dusts herself off*) No, no, I was just trying to get off the beach. It can be pretty tricky sometimes. (*a pause, she looks at her watch.*) Oh, no, I've got to go . . . ! (*She retrieves her purse.*)

LEO. (*following her*) Baby, don't.

HOLLY. Oh God. . . . (*She faces him, motionless*)

LEO. Don't . . .

HOLLY. (*starts to cry*) I've got to, I've *got* to . . . ! Don't look so sad, I can't bear it . . . (*She puts her arms around him, weeping*) Let me go. Please let me go . . . (*She kisses him, then wrenches away and runs off.*) (*a silence*)

LEO. YOUR SHOES . . . ! (*He follows her a few steps holding them up.*)

HAMILTON. I had no idea she was so attractive.

M.J. (*leaning over*) You dropped something dear. What is this? (*She picks it up.*)

HAMILTON. There's always been alot of looks in that family. Her mother was a beauty.

LEO. (*still holding her shoes*) Holly . . .

M.J. A toy shovel.

HAMILTON. Mabel's no slouch either.

M.J. (*dropping the shovel into her bag*) Well, this will

come in handy in the garden. Waste not, want not. (*a silence*)

HAMILTON. Wake up, M.J., we've got alot of work to do. (*to LEO*) Today's our anniversary.

M.J. Don't ask us which one, we've lost count.

HAMILTON. (*starting to open the umbrella part of their tent*) Every year we come down here and have a little celebration, al fresco.

M.J. Poor Hammy, it's really not worth the effort.

HAMILTON. Now, now, you say that every year, but once everything's all set up, you change your tune. (*He digs the umbrella deep into the sand.*)

M.J. But look at you, you're like Lawrence of Arabia!

HAMILTON. Nothing ventured, nothing gained.

M.J. (*to LEO*) Do you believe it . . . ? The man's over 70 and he still carries on like a three year old!

HAMILTON. Quit your yipping M.J., and help me with this stuff.

LEO. (*still holding HOLLY'S shoes, suddenly races up his chair and leans out over the railing*) HOLLY, HOLLY. . . . (*HAMILTON and M.J. stop and look up at him.*)

M.J. Poor thing. (*Looking away*) I can't look.

LEO. (*racing around the railing*) HOLLY WAIT . . . ! COME BACK!

M.J. (*unable to move*), Oh Hammy . . . ! (*A silence*)

HAMILTON. (*Fussing with his gear*) These young people are always losing things. They can't hold onto anything.

M.J. Remember what I put you through the day before our wedding . . . ? Took off on a steamship for Portugal, I was so terrified.

HAMILTON. You were slippery all right.

M.J. I almost made it too if it hadn't been for my

wretched sister spilling the beans . . . I've never for-
given her for it!

HAMILTON. (*unfurling the bolt of material*) O.K.,
M.J., now give me a hand with this. Come on and grab
the other end . . .

M.J. (*She does.*) Right, right. . . .

HAMILTON. Atta girl . . .

M.J. O.K., I've got it . . .

HAMILTON. (*starting to unravel the bolt*) Here we
go . . .

M.J. Careful now. . . .

HAMILTON. I'll just look for the other end here. . . .

M.J. Take it nice and slow. Remember what happened
the last time . . . (*Poor HAMILTON makes a worse
and worse mess of it, getting all tangled up in the volumi-
nous fabric.*)

HAMILTON. HEY THERE, LEO, WANT TO GIVE
US A HAND WITH THIS . . . ? THE DAMNED
STUFF'S GOT A MIND OF ITS OWN! (*He inadver-
tantly pulls M.J. off balance with his flailings*)

M.J. (*goes flying*) LOOK OUT, LOOK OUT!

HAMILTON. For pity's sake, M.J., what *are* you
doing . . . ?!

M.J. What am *I* doing . . . ? *You're* the one that's
yanking me all over kingdom come!

HAMILTON. Look, all you have to do is hang on to
your end while I. . . .

M.J. That's easy for *you* to say. . . .

HAMILTON. COME ON THERE LEO, LET'S GET
CRACKING!

LEO. Yes . . . ?

HAMILTON. Could you give us a hand here? (*He pulls
on his end again.*)

M.J. (*tottering*) Hammy, *please*!

HAMILTON. GODDAMNED CHEESECLOTH!

M.J. (*to LEO, who's come down from his chair*) We go through this every year . . . every year.

HAMILTON. (*to M.J.*) If you could just do what I asked you. . . .

M.J. Sweetheart, I'm trying!

LEO. O.K., let's see what the problem is. (*He takes the material from M.J.*) May I . . . ?

M.J. (*to HAMILTON*) Really darling, don't you think we're getting too old for this!

HAMILTON. (*putting his arm around her*) Speak for yourself, Madame! (*LEO starts hanging the gauze as they watch.*)

M.J. Oh, Leo, what would we do without you?

HAMILTON. I hate to think.

LEO. Oh, you'd manage.

M.J. (*gazing at the tent*) It's amazing how well it's stood up after all these years.

HAMILTON. Remember the summer we lugged it down to Singing Beach?

M.J. (*laughing*) Oh God!

HAMILTON. The whole thing collapsed on us when the tide came in!

M.J. (*to LEO*) You should have seen it! We looked like a couple of parachutists who'd just come in for a crash landing!

HAMILTON. (*admiring LEO'S handiwork*) Ahhhh, looking good, looking good.

M.J. I always forget how handsome it is once it's up.

HAMILTON. (*to M.J.*) "In Xanadu, did Kubla Khan, a stately pleasure dome decree . . . "

M.J. "Where Alph, the sacred river ran, through caverns measureless to man, down to a sunless sea."

LEO. There we go, that should do it.

M.J. I don't know how to thank you.

HAMILTON. (*heading into the tent*) O.K., M.J., I've got the table and chairs. Let's get this show on the road. (*HAMILTON starts setting them up as M.J. gathers the food.*)

HAMILTON. And the lantern . . . don't forget the lantern!

M.J. Right you are. Vouloir c'est pouvoir! (*She sets the lantern on the table and turns it on. (to LEO)* Would you care to join us for a little drink . . . ?

HAMILTON. Yes, do!

LEO. Oh, no thanks, No thanks.

M.J. (*leaving the tent and coming up to him*) We'd love to have you, really!

LEO. That's very kind of you, but. . . .

HAMILTON. Come on, there's plenty of champagne.

M.J. Oh, *do* join us!

LEO. No, no, another time. Really . . .

HAMILTON. You're sure?

LEO. Yeah.

M.J. Well, don't feel you have to stick around on our account.

HAMILTON. Yes, please don't let us interfere with your plans.

LEO. That's O.K., I feel like sitting awhile. (*He heads back up to his perch.*)

HAMILTON. (*holding the tent flap open*) Come on, M.J., get a wiggle on. . . .

M.J. I'm coming, I'm coming. . . .

HAMILTON. . . . . the mosquitos are going to eat us alive!

M.J. (*scurrying inside*) Hold your horses, I've only got three hands.

HAMILTON. Atta girl.

M.J. (*collapsing into her chair*) Uuugh, honestly darling!

HAMILTON. (*sitting in his*) There, this is more like it! (*starts rummaging around for the champagne*) O.K.. . . . Upward and onward. . . .

M.J. (*setting up the glasses*) Upward and onward. . . .

HAMILTON. What a night, what a night!

M.J. Good old Hammy, the last of the romantics.

HAMILTON. Smell that air! (*The little tent glows merrily against the darkening sky as M.J. and HAMILTON set up their feast.*)

M.J. How many years *has* it been . . . ? (*The lights start to fade around them, leaving LEO in an afterglow. He gazes wistfully at their tent, suddenly rising. He then pulls HOLLY'S number out of his pocket and slowly recites it to himself, breaking into a radiant smile.*)

LEO. Oh yes!

AS THE CURTAIN SLOWLY FALLS

COSTUME PLOT

Andre
Suit (3 piece)
Shirt
Tie
Snazzy Italian shoes
Raincoat
White scarf
Umbrella

Faith
Denim jumper
Four tee shirts
Bathing suit
Preg. pad
Yellow and white striped jacket
Tan poplin jacket
Jumpsuit
Pastel plain shorts
Long sleeved striped shirt
The crazy sweater Ariel made her
Shorts
Hat

Ariel
Bathing suit
Pullover
Sweater
Wrap kimono
Green tee shirt
Gold with peach silk top (sleeveless)
Silk patchwork jacket
Green visor

Hamilton
Baseball cap
Beat up Brooks Brothers sport shirt
Poplin jacket
2 short sleeved shirts
Poplin pants
Ancient Swim trunks
White formal jacket
Black formal pants
White formal shirt
Black cumerbund
Black bow tie

Holly
White baseball cap
2 white tee shirts
Turquoise tee shirt
Wrap shorts
Pink sun dress
2 royal blue tee shirts
2 black shorts
Lifeguard sweatshirt
White cotton sweater
Earrings
Bracelet
Jumpsuit
Belt
High heel sandals
Mohair sweater
Jeans
Purse
White gauze skirt

Leo
Helmet

Sunglasses
Orange trunks (two pair)
Running shorts
2 grey tee shirts
Blue jeans
Wind breaker
Lifeguard sweatshirt

M.J.
Beach hat
Bathing suit
Pullover
Evening wear
Striped awning jacket
Rayon pants
V-neck tee shirt
Pants
Striped shirt

Miranda
Bathing suit
Cotton tops
White shorts
Blue shorts
Sweatshirt
Ragg wool sweater

Winston
Swimming trunks
Sweatshirt
Shorts
Tee shirts
Hooded sweatshirt
Sweatpants

PROPS

Tons of sand
Ocean, or the illusion of ocean
Lifeguard stand
Beach umbrellas
Towels and quilts
Pails, shovels and castle molds
Picnic baskets
Folding chairs
Folding table
Suntan lotion
Candy and food
Shells and brain coral
Thermoses
Plates and glasses
Champagne and iced tea
Carrying bags filled with extra sweaters, bathingsuits,
    paperbacks, things from home
Crocheting yarn and needles
Playing cards
Quentin Bell's biography of Virginia Woolf
The Boston Globe
M.J.'s paints and completed water colors
Sunglasses and baby oil
Lifeguard's whistle
Tripod
Classy 35 mm camera
Beached whale
Bluber
Tin can telephones
First aid kit
Blood bag and tweezers
Bactine

Disappearing bouquet or flock of doves
Umbrella-type tent
Yards of bleached gauze
Gallery invitation
Beat up brass lantern

Author's Notes on the Setting

There's something wonderfully audacious about setting a play on a beach. Since the audience is sitting *indoors,* major trickery is called for. The key is embracing it with high spirits. It's all just a matter of illusion. Only four elements are needed, and none of them cost very much —sand, scrim, paint and light. The amount of sand you'll need will depend on the size of your stage. (Six tons at The Second Stage vs. 20 at the much larger arena space of Circle in the Square, for example). Be sure to hollow out several pits, one so Holly can be buried, and others to accommodate beach umbrella poles and the tent at the end. Also, the sand must be watered down before each performance so the actors won't sneeze or choke to death. The real challenge of the design is capturing the movement of the beach because the weather and time of day are always changing. One scene takes place at dawn, another on a dappled afternoon, the next during a violent thunderstorm. The restlessness of the ocean and sky have to read on dry land. Of couse the actors are a great help in *playing* it all, but finally it's paint, light, fabric and imagination that make it real.

T. H.

CEMENTVILLE
by Jane Martin
Comedy
Little Theatre

(5m., 9f.) Int. The comic sensation of the 1991 Humana Festival at the famed Actors Theatre of Louisville, this wildly funny new play by the mysterious author of *Talking With* and *Vital Signs* is a brilliant portrayal of America's fascination with fantasy entertainment, "the growth industry of the 90's." We are in a run-down locker room in a seedy sports arena in the Armpit of the Universe, "Cementville, Tennessee," with the scurviest bunch of professional wrasslers you ever saw. This is decidedly a small-time operation—not the big time you see on TV. The promoter, Bigman, also appears in the show. He and his brother Eddie are the only men, though; for the main attraction(s) are the "ladies." There's Tiger, who comes with a big drinking problem and a small dog; Dani, who comes with a large chip on her shoulder against Bigman, who owes all the girls several weeks' pay; Lessa, an ex-Olympic shotputter with delusions that she is actually employed presently in athletics; and Netty, an overweight older woman who appears in the ring dressed in baggy pajamas, with her hair in curlers, as the character "Pajama Mama." There is the eager-beaver go-fer Nola, a teenager who dreams of someday entering the glamorous world of pro wrestling herself. And then, there are the Knockout Sisters, refugees from the Big Time but banned from it for heavy-duty abuse of pharmaceuticals as well as having gotten arrested *in flagrante delicto* with the Mayor of Los Angeles. They have just gotten out of the slammer; but their indefatigable manager, Mother Crocker ("Of the Auto-Repair Crockers") hopes to get them reinstated, if she can keep them off the white powder. Bigman has hired the Knockout Sisters as tonight's main attraction, and the fur really flies along with the sparks when the other women find out about the Knockout Sisters. Bigman has really got his hands full tonight. He's gotta get the girls to tear each other up in the ring, not the locker room; he's gotta deal with tough-as-nails Mother Crocker; he's gotta keep an arena full of tanked-up rubes from tearing up the joint—and he's gotta solve the mystery of who bit off his brother Eddie's dick last night.   (#5580)

XXXXXXXXXXXXXXXXXXXXXXXXXXXX
BURIED TREASURE FROM SAMUEL
FRENCH, INC.

Most of the superb plays listed below have never been produced in
New York City. Does this mean they aren't "good enough" for
New York? JUDGE FOR YOURSELF!

ABOUT FACE -- AN ACT OF THE IMAGINATION -- ALL SHE
CARES ABOUT IS THE YANKEES -- ALONE AT THE BEACH --
AMERICAN CANTATA -- THE ANASTASIA FILE --
ARCHANGELS DON'T PLAY PINBALL -- THE BAR OFF
MELROSE -- BEDROOMS -- BEYOND REASONABLE DOUBT --
BILL W. AND DR. BOB -- BINGO -- BLUE COLLAR BLUES --
BODYWORK -- BRONTE -- CARELESS LOVE -- CAT'S PAW --
CHEKHOV IN YALTA -- A CHORUS OF DISAPPROVAL --
CINCINNATI -- THE CURATE SHAKESPEARE AS YOU LIKE
IT -- DADDY'S DYIN' -- DANCERS -- DARKSIDE --
ELIZABETH -- FIGHTING CHANCE -- FOOLIN' AROUND
WITH INFINITY -- GETTING THE GOLD -- GILLETTE -- THE
GIRLHOOD OF SHAKESPEARE'S HEROINES -- GOD'S
COUNTRY --- IMAGINARY LINES -- INTERPRETERS --
LLOYD'S PRAYER -- MAKE IN BANGKOK -- MORE FUN
THAN BOWLING -- OWNERS -- PAPERS -- PIZZA MAN --
POSTMORTEM -- PRAVDA -- THE PUPPETMASTER OF LODZ -
THE REAL QUEEN OF HEARTS AIN'T EVEN PRETTY -- RED
NOSES -- RETROFIT -- RETURN ENGAGEMENTS -- THE
RIVERS AND RAVINES -- ROBIN HOOD -- SHIVAREE -- A
SMALL FAMILY BUSINESS -- STAINED GLASS -- TAKE A
PICTURE -- TALES FROM HOLLYWOOD -- TEN NOVEMBER --
THEATER TRIP -- THIS ONE THING I DO -- THIS SAVAGE
PARADE -- TRAPS -- THE VOICE OF THE PRAIRIE --
WIDOW'S WEEDS -- THE WISTERIA BUSH -- THE WOMAN
IN BLACK

Consult our most recent Catalogue for details.
XXXXXXXXXXXXXXXXXXXXXXXXXXXX

RAVENSCROFT. (Little Theatre.) Mystery. Don Nigro. 1m., 5f. Simple unit set. This unusual play is several cuts above the genre it explores, a Gothic thriller for groups that don't usually do such things, a thinking person's mystery, a dark comedy that is at times immensely funny and at others quite frightening. On a snowy night, Inspector Ruffing is called to a remote English country house to investigate the headlong plunge of a young manservant, Patrick Roarke, down the main staircase, and finds himself getting increasingly involved in the lives of five alluring and dangerous women— Marcy, the beautiful Viennese governess with a past, Mrs. Ravenscroft, the flirtatious and chattery lady of the manor, Gillian, her charming but possibly demented daughter, Mrs. French, the formidable and passionate cook, and Dolly, a frantic and terrified little maid—who lead him through an increasingly bewildering labyrinth of contradictory versions of what happened to Patrick and to the dead Mr. Ravenscroft before him. There are ghosts at the top of the staircase, skeletons in the closet, and much more than the Inspector had bargained for as his quest to solve one mystery leads him deeper and deeper into others and to an investigation of his own tortured soul and the nature of truth itself. You will not guess the ending, but you will be teased, seduced, bewildered, amused, frightened and led along with the Inspector to a dark encounter with truth, or something even stranger. A funny, first rate psychological mystery, and more.

(#19987)

DARK SONNETS OF THE LADY, THE. (Advanced Groups.) Drama. Don Nigro. 4m., 4f. Unit set. First produced professionally at the McCarter Theatre in Princeton and a finalist for the National Play Award, this stunningly theatrical and very funny drama takes place in Vienna in the fall of the year 1900, when Dora, a beautiful and brilliant young girl, walks into the office of Sigmund Freud, then an obscure doctor in his forties, to begin the most famous and controversial encounter in the history of psychoanalysis. Dora is funny, suspicious, sarcastic and elusive, and Freud become fascinated and obsessed by her and by the intricate labyrinth of her illness. He moves like a detective through the mystery of her life, and we meet in the course of his journey through her mind: her lecherous father, her obsessively house-cleaning mother, her irritating brother, her sinister admirer Herr Klippstein and his sensual and seductive wife, and their pretty and lost little governess. Nightmares, fantasies, hallucinations and memories all come alive onstage in a wild kaleidoscopic tapestry as Freud moves closer and closer to the truth about Dora's murky past, and the play becomes a kind of war between the two of them about what the truth is, about the uneasy truce between men and women, and ultimately a tragic love story. Laced throughout with eerie and haunting Strauss waltzes, this is a rich, complex, challenging and delightfully intriguing universe, a series of riddles one inside the other that lead the audience step by step to the center of Dora's troubled soul and her innermost secrets. Is Dora sick, or is the corrupt patriarchal society in which she and Freud are both trapped the real source of a complex group neurosis that binds all the characters together in a dark web of desperate erotic relationships, a kind of beautiful, insane and terrible dance of life, desire and death?

(#5952)

TWO NEW COMEDIES FROM
━━━━━━ SAMUEL FRENCH, Inc.━━━━━━

FAST GIRLS. (Little Theatre). Comedy. Diana Amsterdam. 2m., 3f. Int. Lucy
Lewis is a contemporary, single woman in her thirties with what used to be called a
"healthy sex life," much to the chagrin of her mother, who feels Lucy is too fast, too
easy—and too single. Her best friend, on the other hand, neighbor Abigail McBride, is
deeply envious of Lucy's ease with men. When Lucy wants to date a man she just calls
him up, whereas Abigail sits home alone waiting for Ernest, who may not even know
she exists, to call. The only time Abigail isn't by the phone is after Lucy has had a hot
date, when she comes over to Lucy's apartment to hear the juicy details and get green
with envy. Sometimes, though, Lucy doesn't want to talk about it, which drives Abigail
nuts ("If you don't tell me about men I have no love life!"). Lucy's mother arrives to
take the bull by the horns, so to speak, arriving with a challenge. Mom claims no man
will marry Lucy (even were she to *want to* get married), because she's too easy. Lucy
takes up the challenge, announcing that she is going to get stalwart ex-boyfriend
Sidney ("we're just friends") Epstein to propose to her. Easier said than done. Sidney
doesn't *want* a fast girl. Maybe dear old Mom is right, thinks Lucy. Maybe fast girls
can't have it all. "Amsterdam makes us laugh, listen and think."—Daily Record.
"Brilliantly comic moments."—The Monitor. "rapidly paced comedy with a load of
laughs . . . a funny entertainment with some pause for reflection on today's [sexual]
confusion."—Suburban News. "Takes a penetrating look at [contemporary sexual
chaos]. Passion, celibacy, marriage, fidelity are just some of the subjects that Diana
Amsterdam hilariously examines."—Tribune News.   (#8149)

ADVICE FROM A CATERPILLAR. (Little Theatre.) Comedy. Douglas
Carter Beane. 2m. 2f. 1 Unit set & 1 Int. Ally Sheedy and Dennis Christopher starred
in the delightful off-Broadway production of this hip new comedy. Ms. Sheedy played
Missy, an avant garde video artist who specializes in re-runs of her family's home
videos, adding her own disparaging remarks. Needless to say, she is very alienated
from the middle-class, family values she grew up with, which makes her very *au
courant*, but strangely unhappy. She has a successful career and a satisfactory love-
life with a businessman named Suit. Suit's married, but that doesn't stop him and
Missy from carrying on. Something's missing, though—and Missy isn't sure what it
is, until she meets Brat. He is a handsome young aspiring actor. Unfortunately, Brat is
also the boyfriend of Missy's best friend. Sound familiar? It isn't—because Missy's
best friend is a gay man named Spaz! Spaz has been urging Missy to find an
unmarried boyfriend, but this is too much—too much for Spaz, too much for Suit and,
possibly, too much for Missy. Does she *want* a serious relationship (ugh—how
bourgeois!)? Can a bisexual unemployed actor actually be her Mr. Wonderful? "Very
funny ... a delightful evening."—Town & Village.   (#3876)